roSS
cartoons

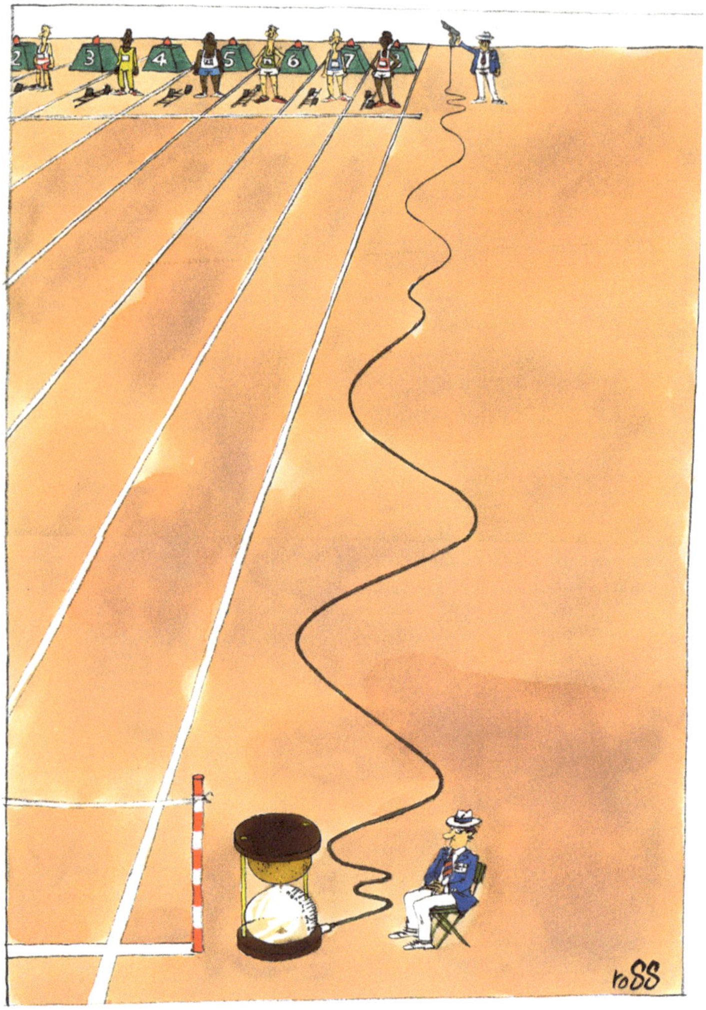
2
3
4
5
6
7
roSS

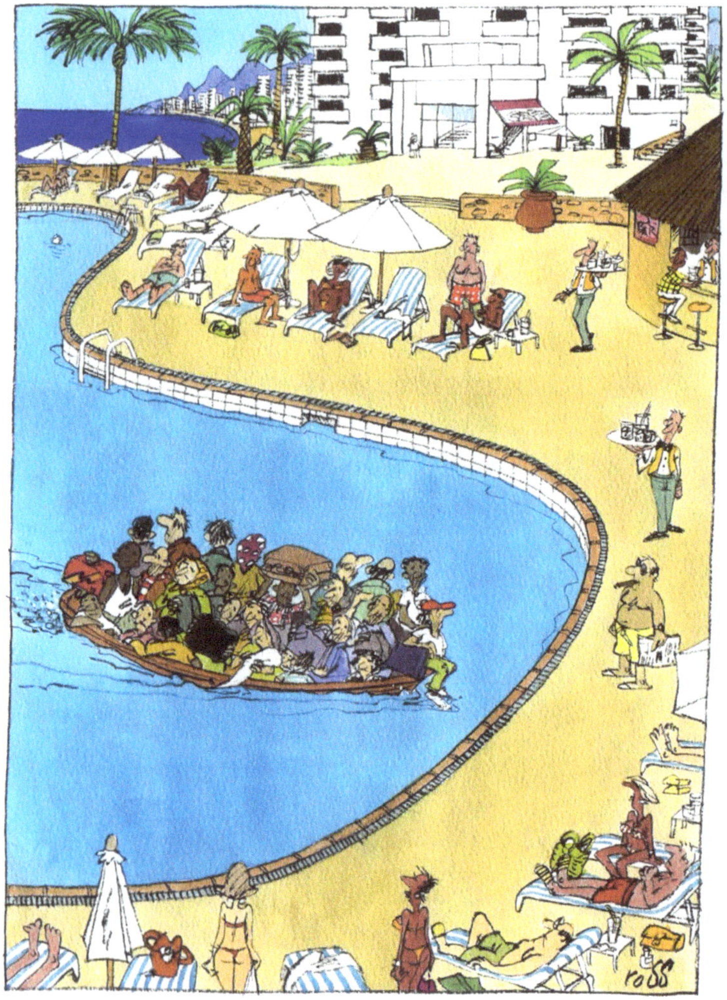
roSS

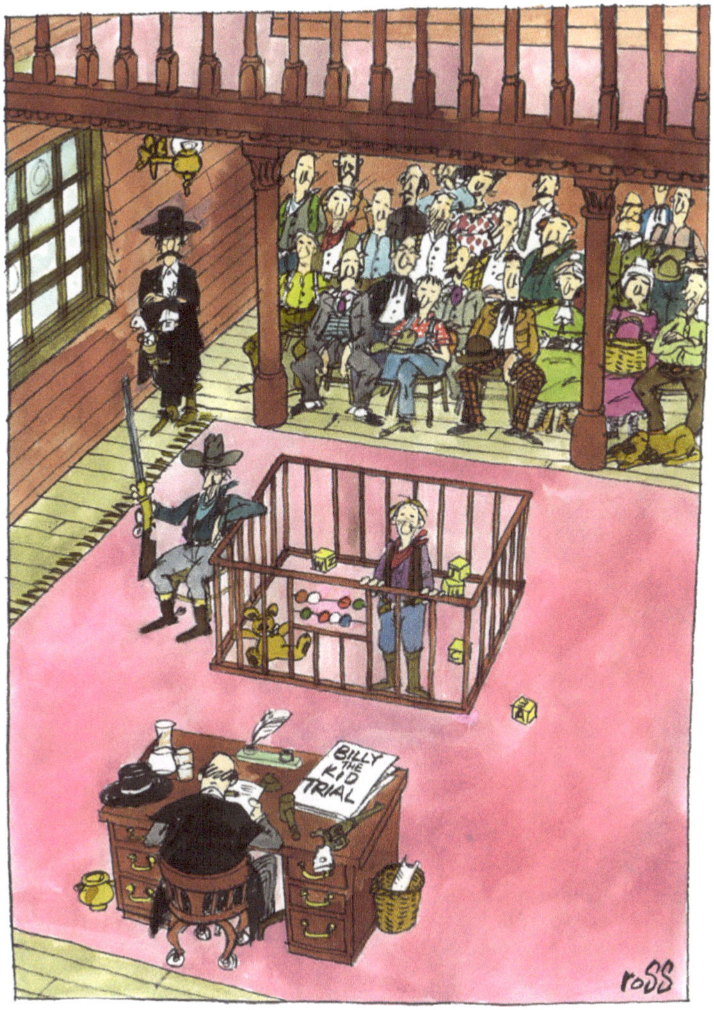
BILLY THE KID TRIAL
roSS

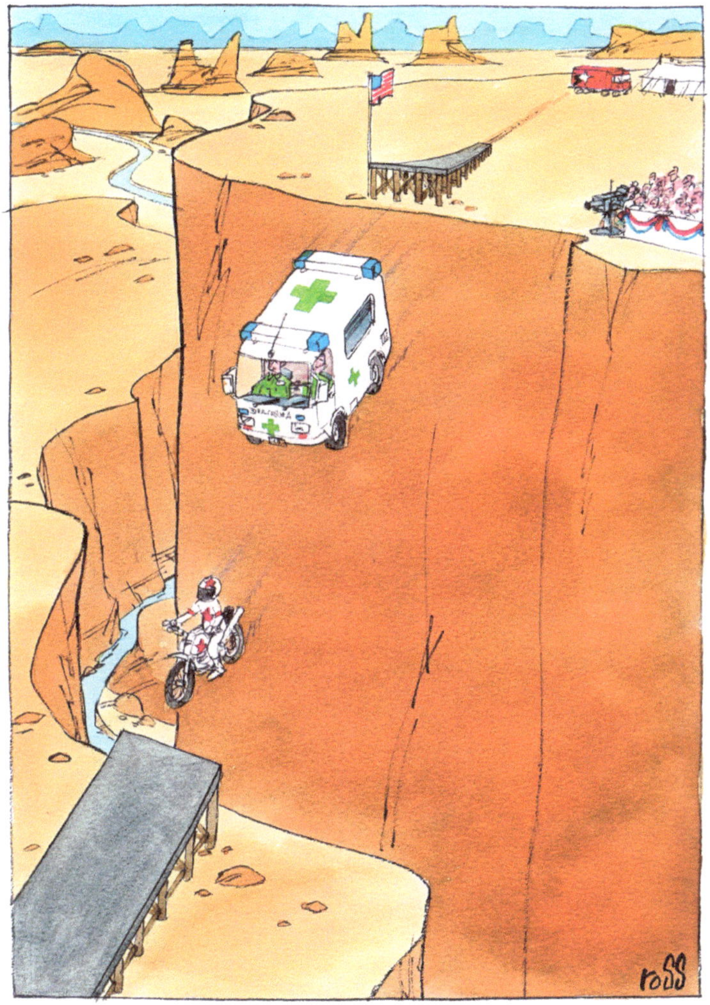
roSS

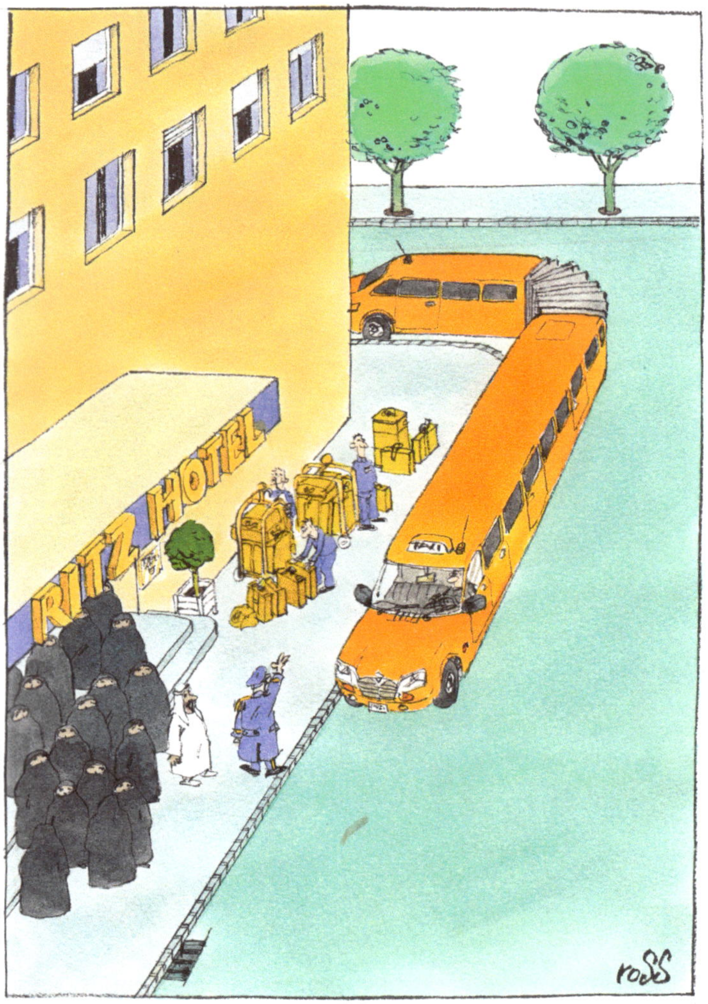
RITZ HOTEL
roSS

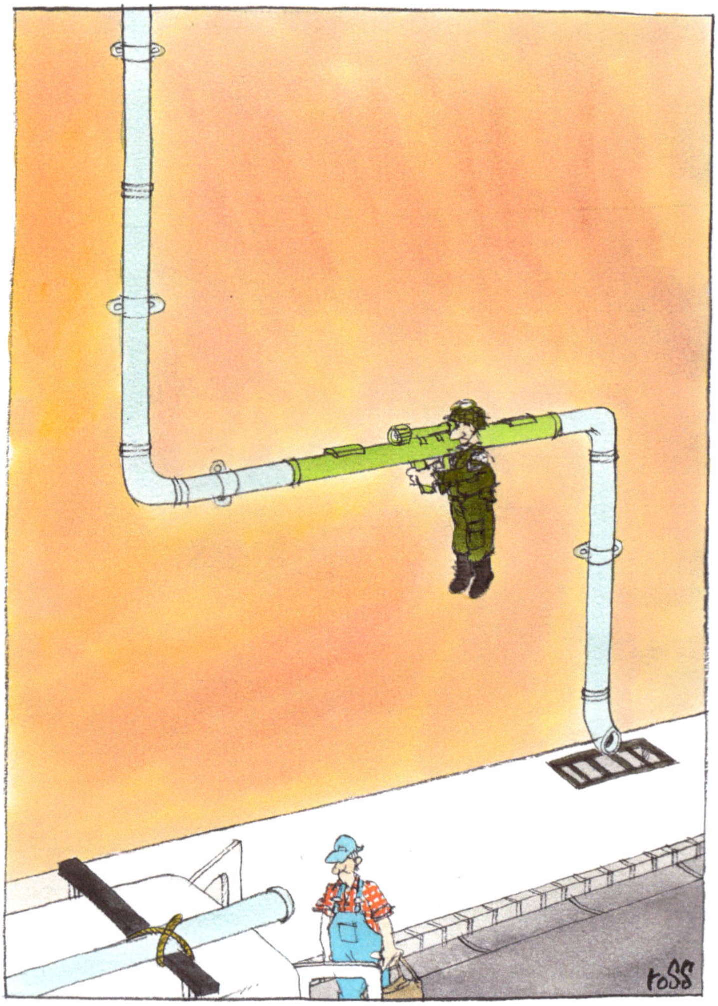
roSS

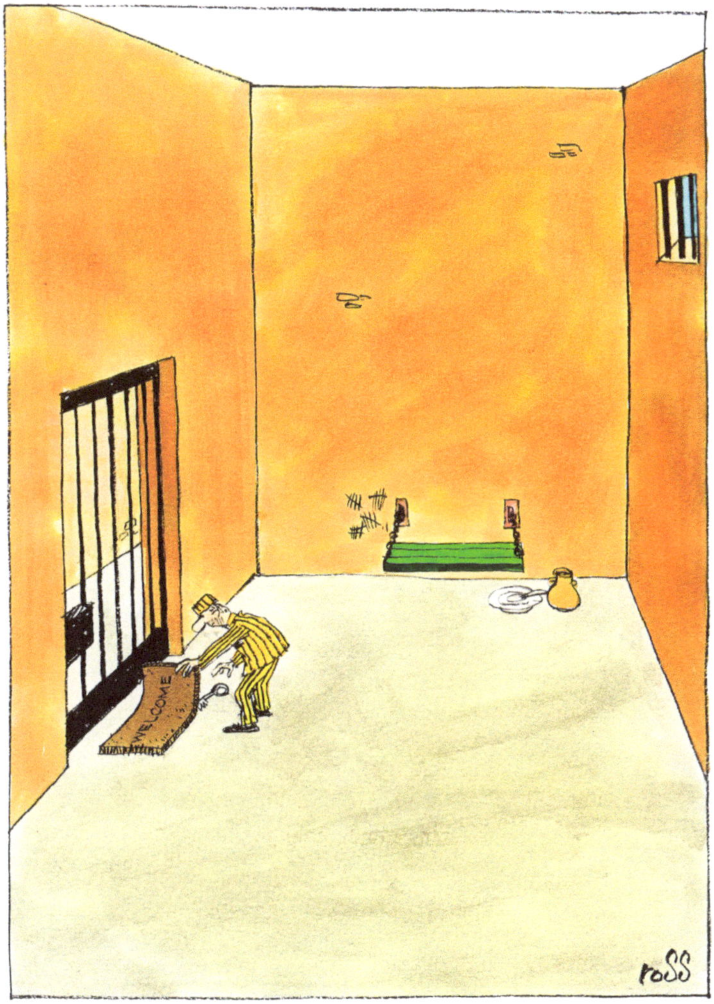
WELCOME
roSS

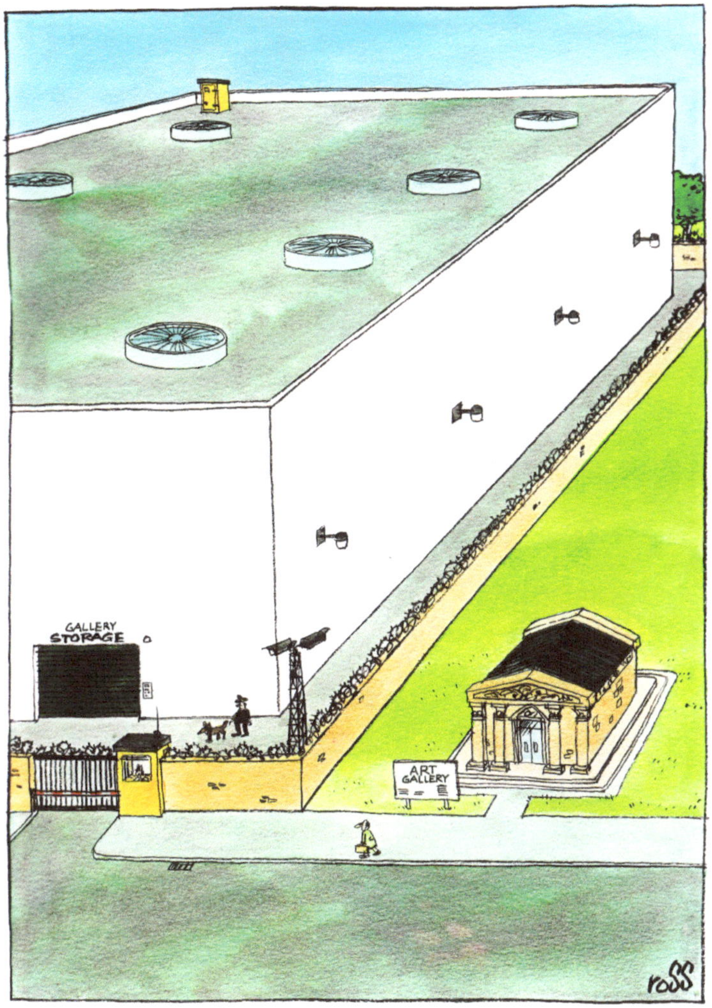
GALLERY
STORAGE
ART
GALLERY
roSS

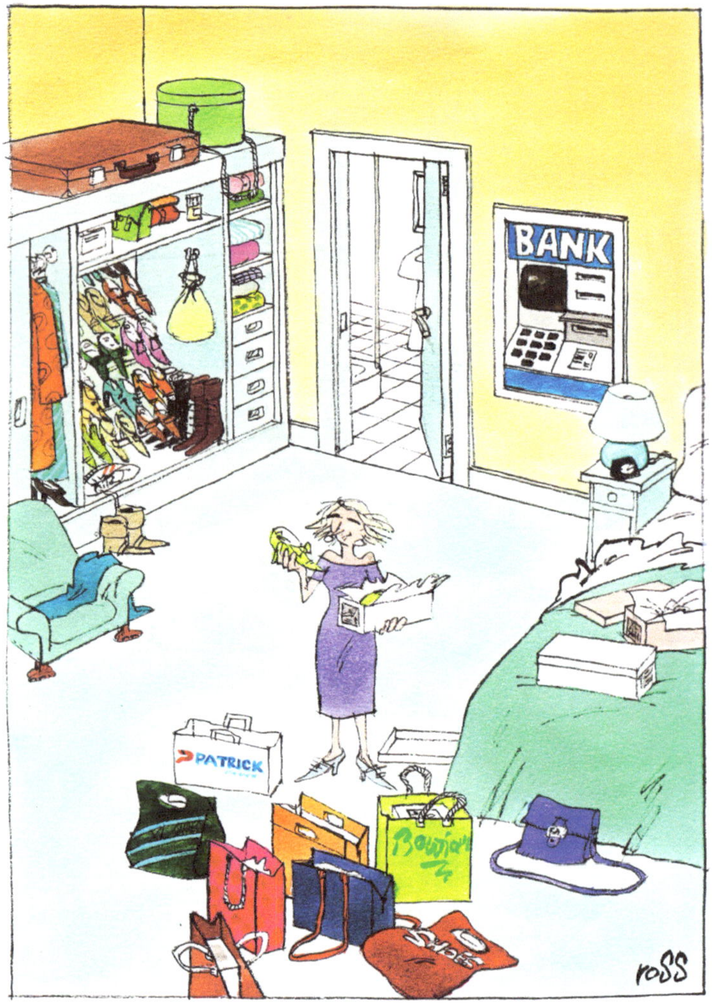
BANK
PATRICK
roSS

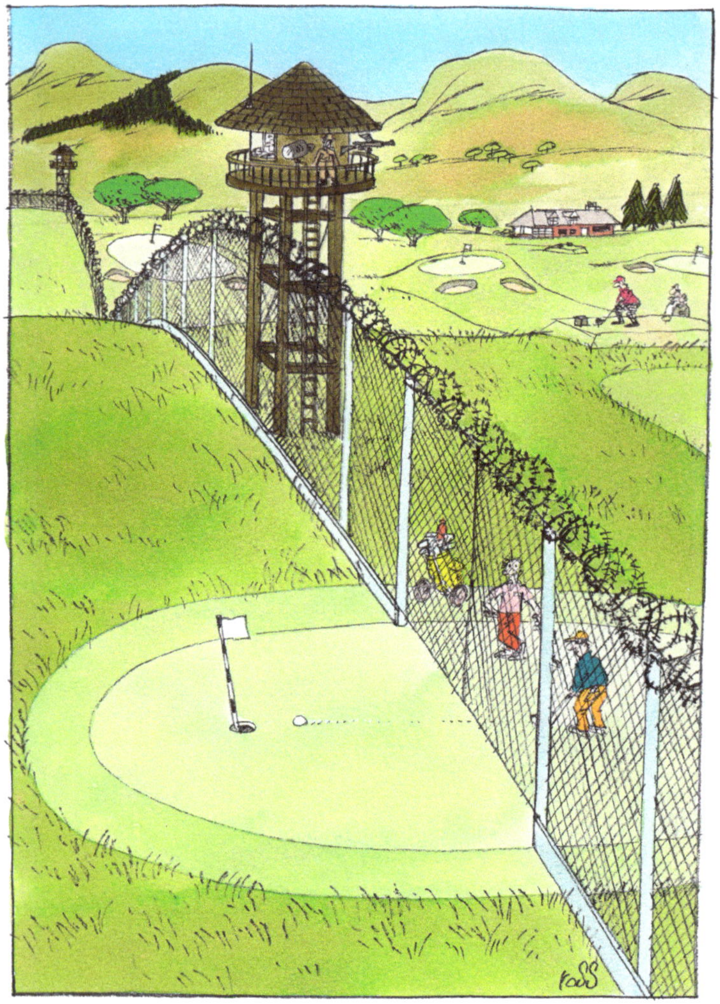
roSS

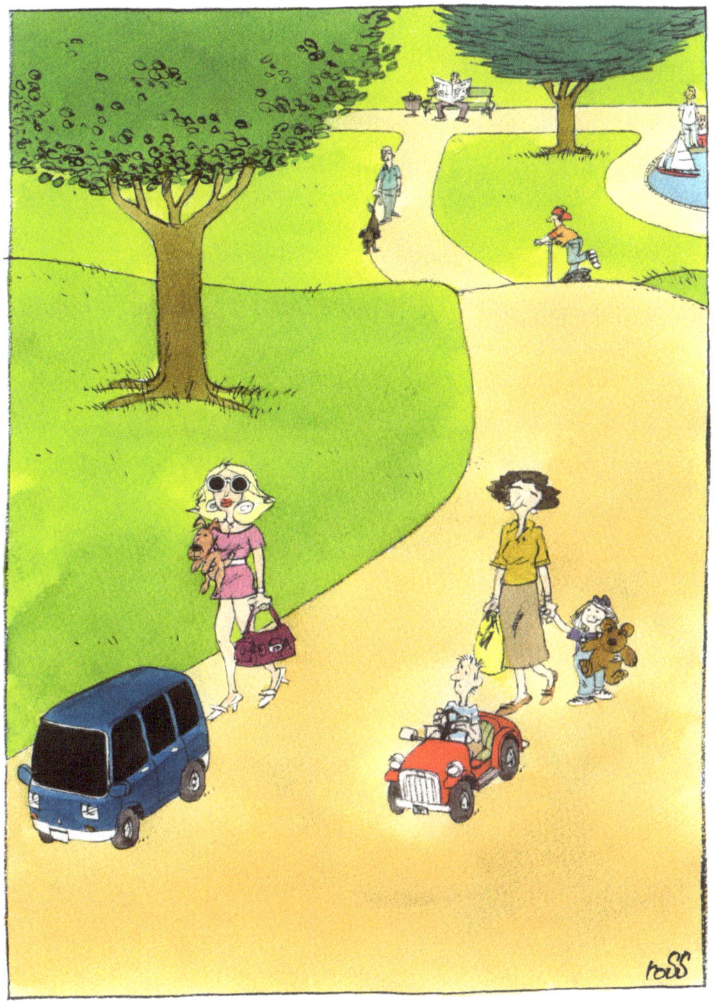
roSS

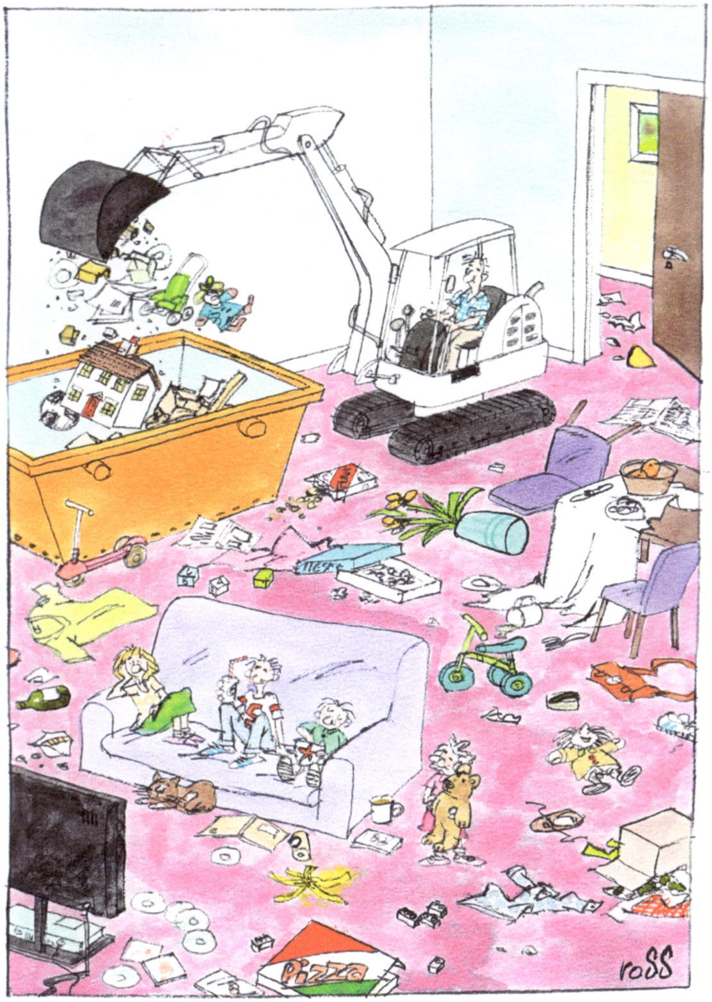
Pizza
roSS

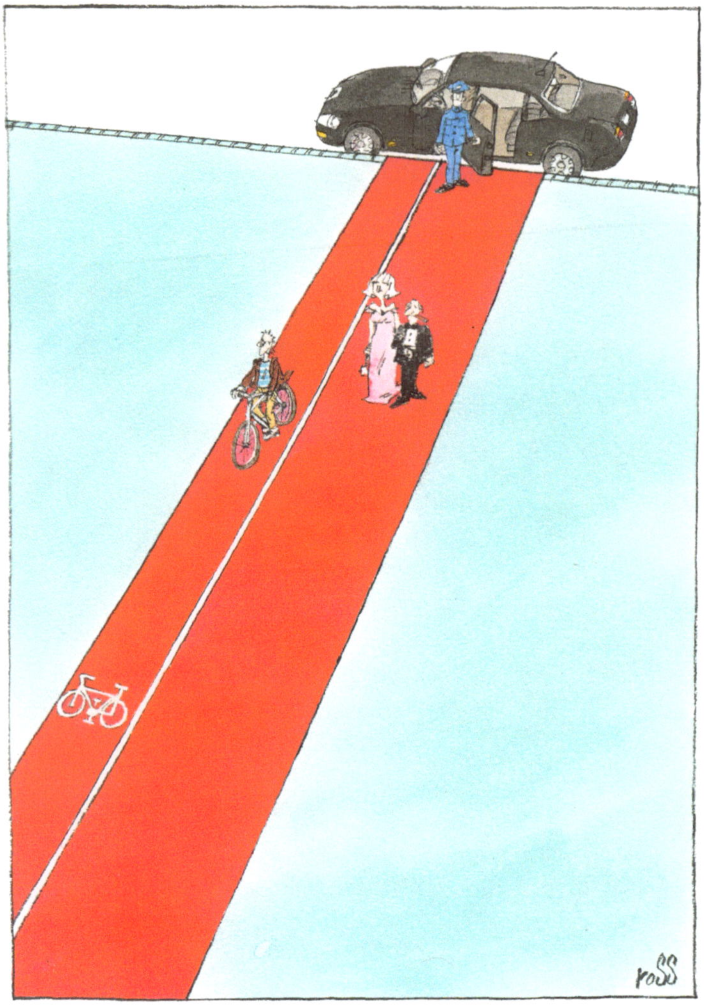
roSS

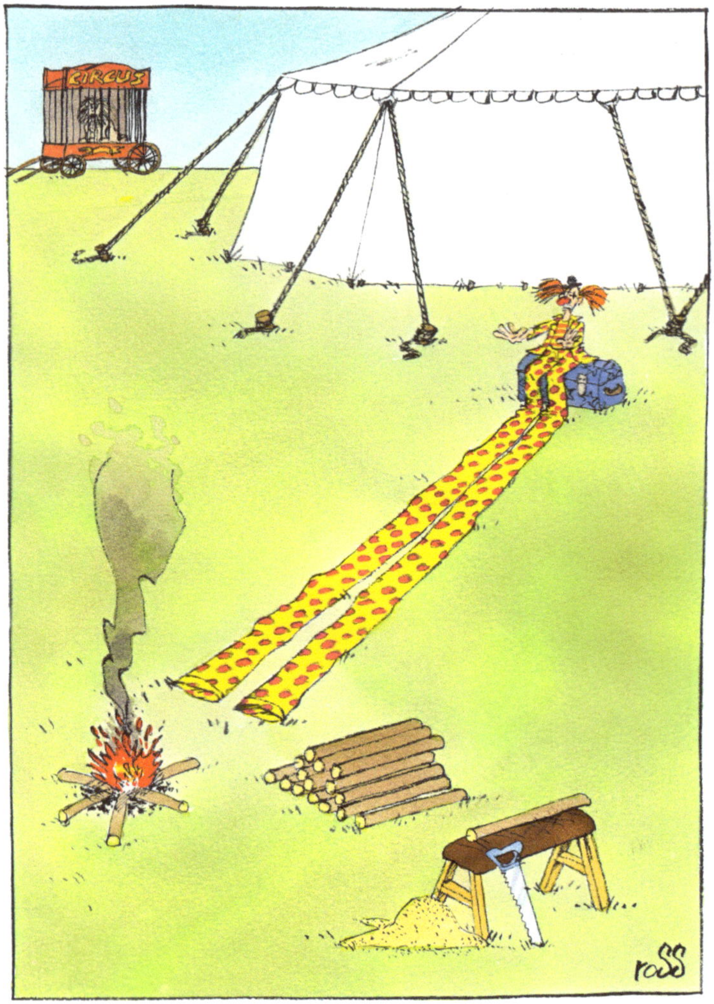
CIRCUS
roSS

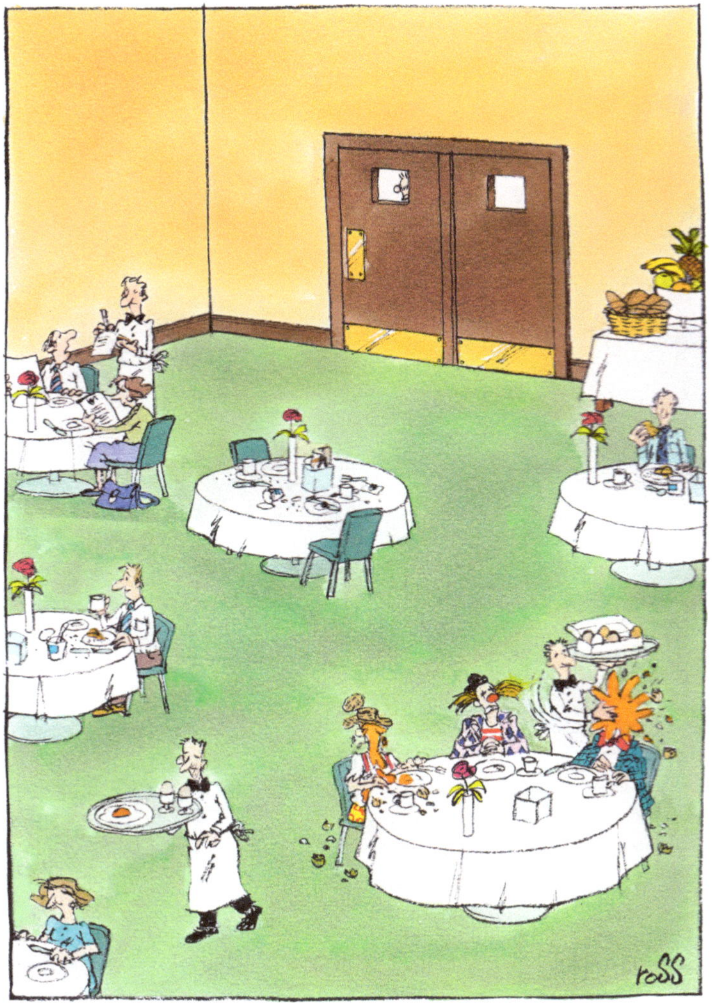
roSS
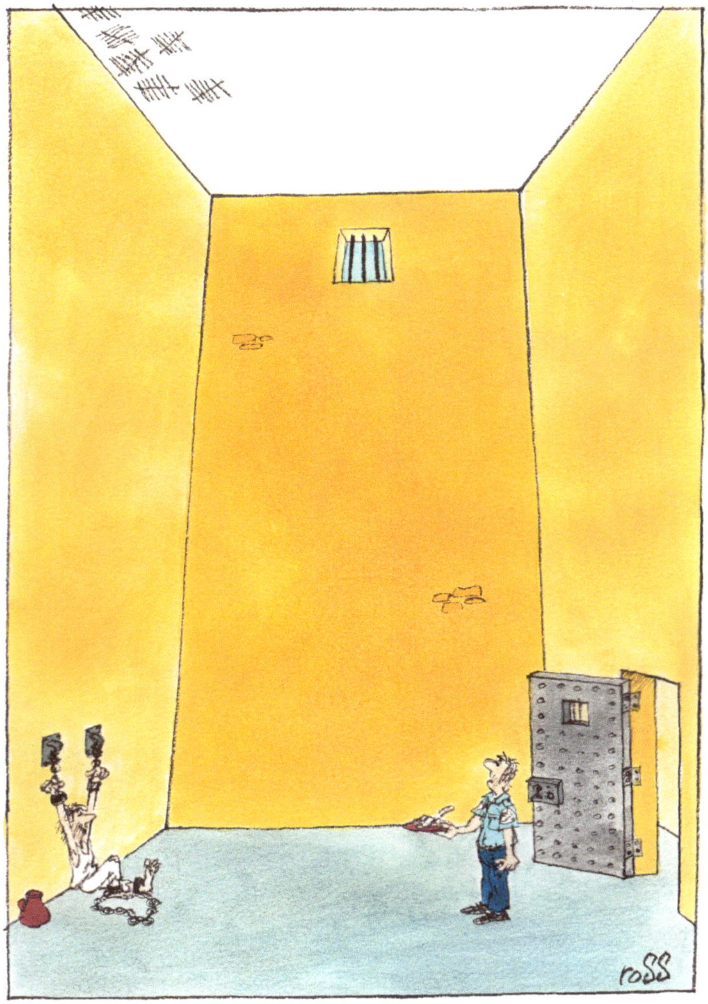
roSS

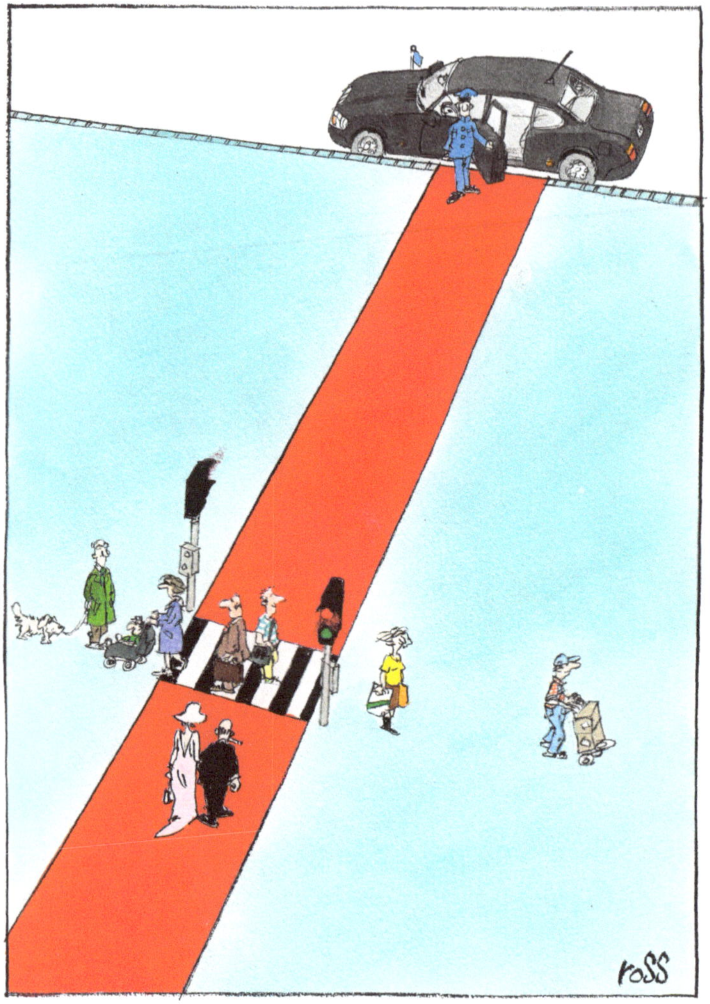
roSS

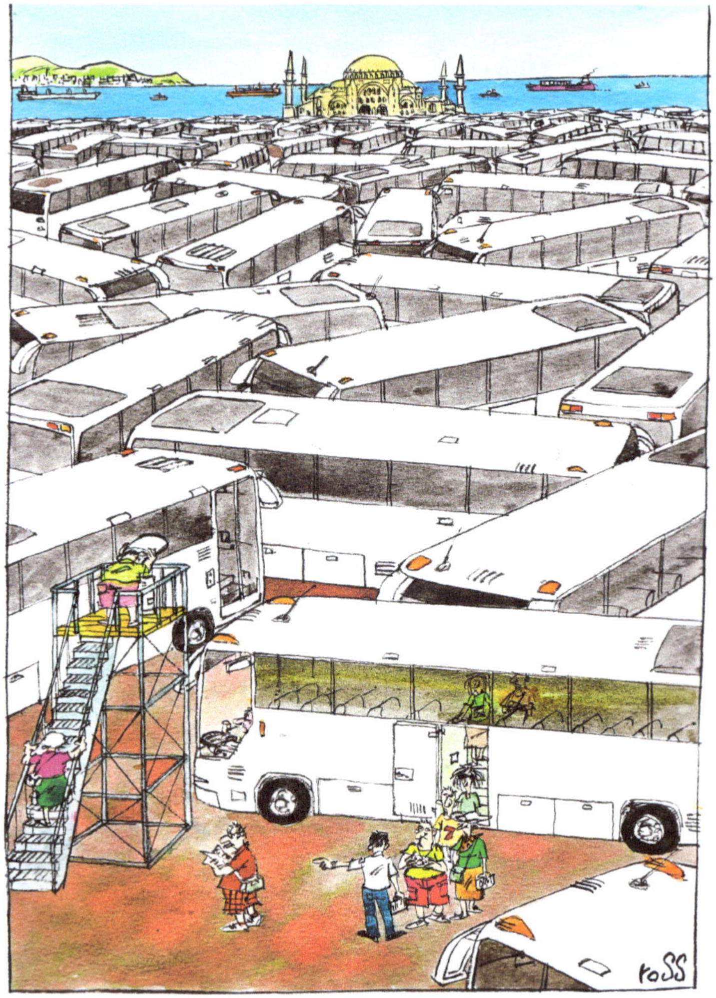
roSS

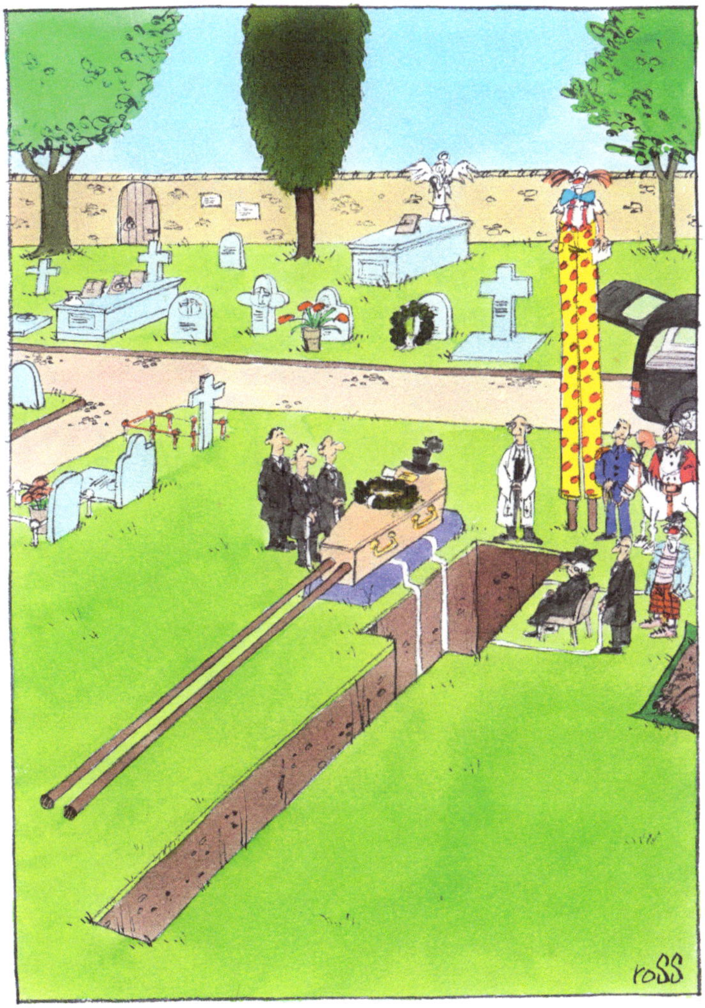
roSS

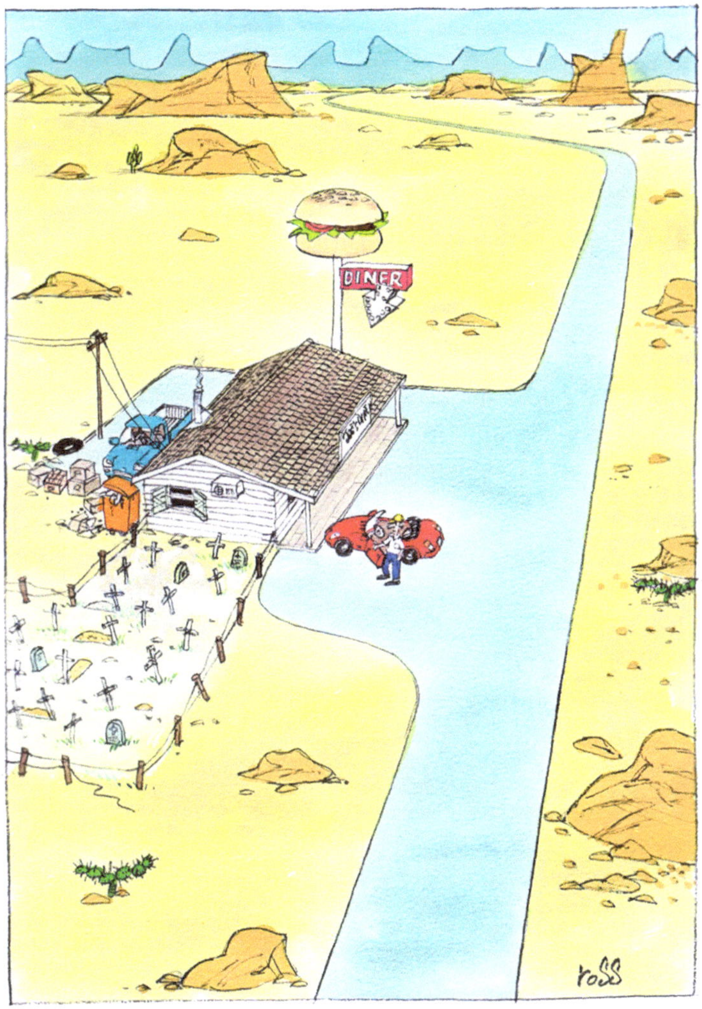
DINER
roSS

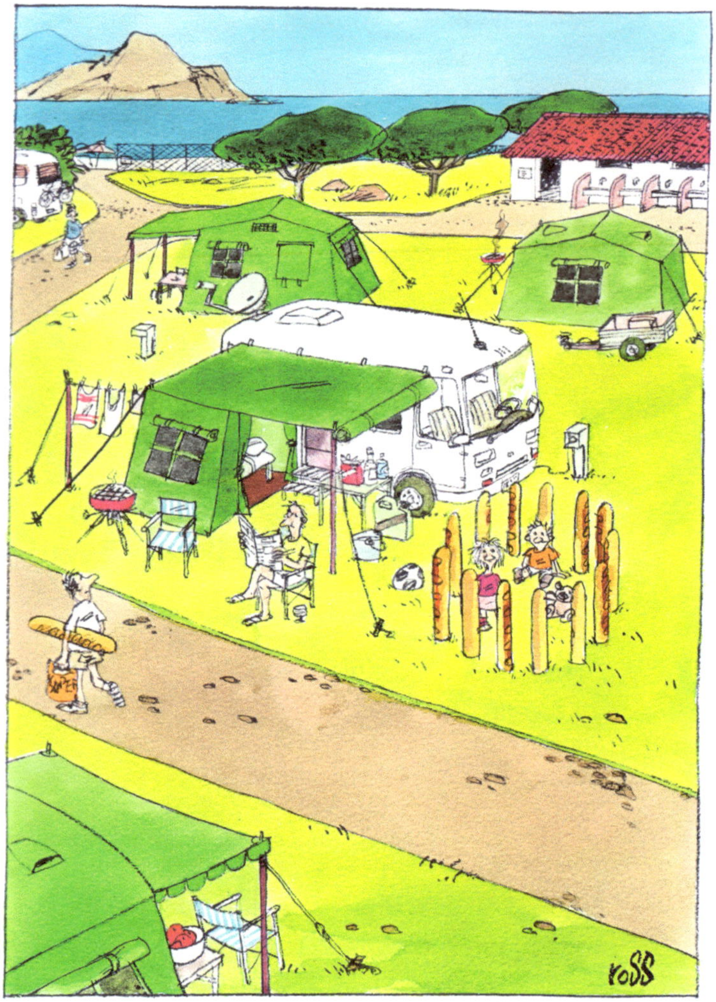
roSS

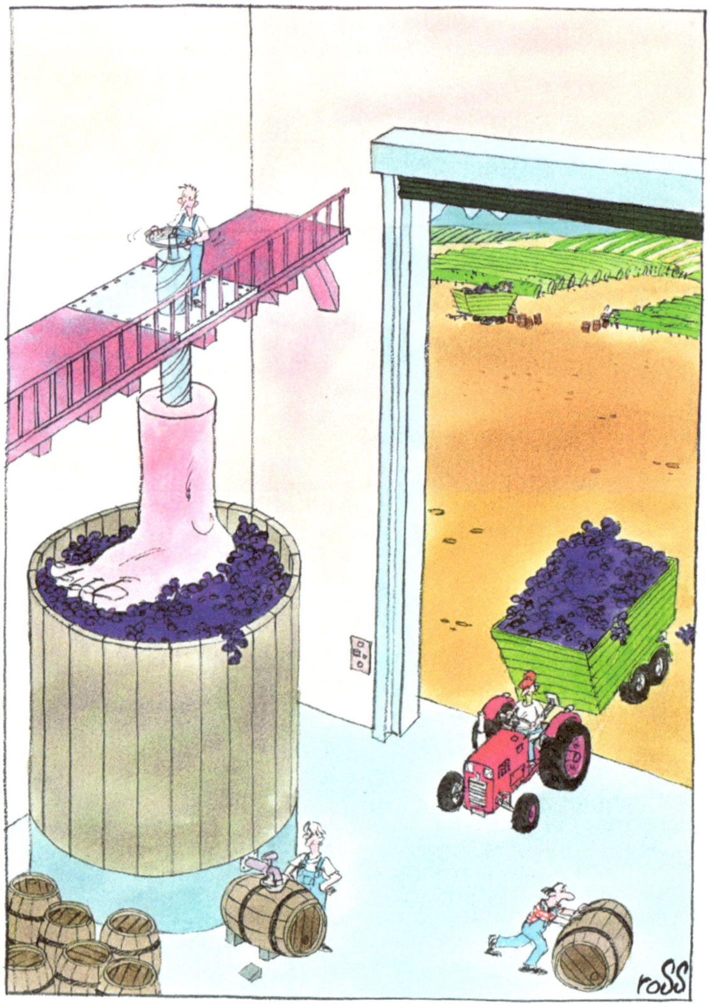
roSS

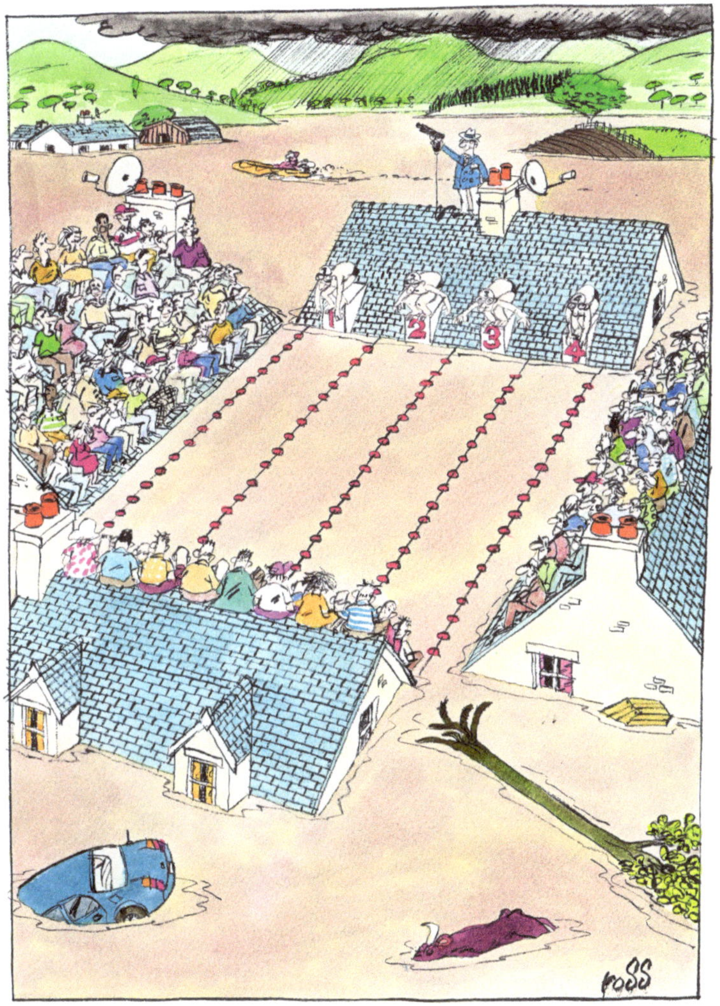
1
2
3
4
roSS

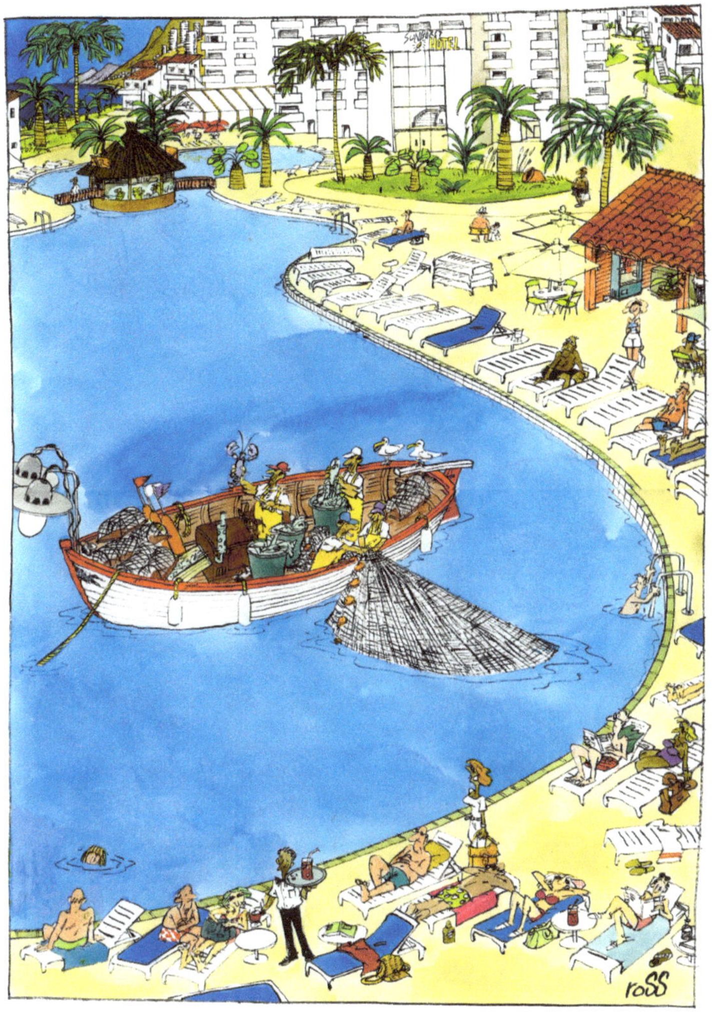
HOTEL
roSS

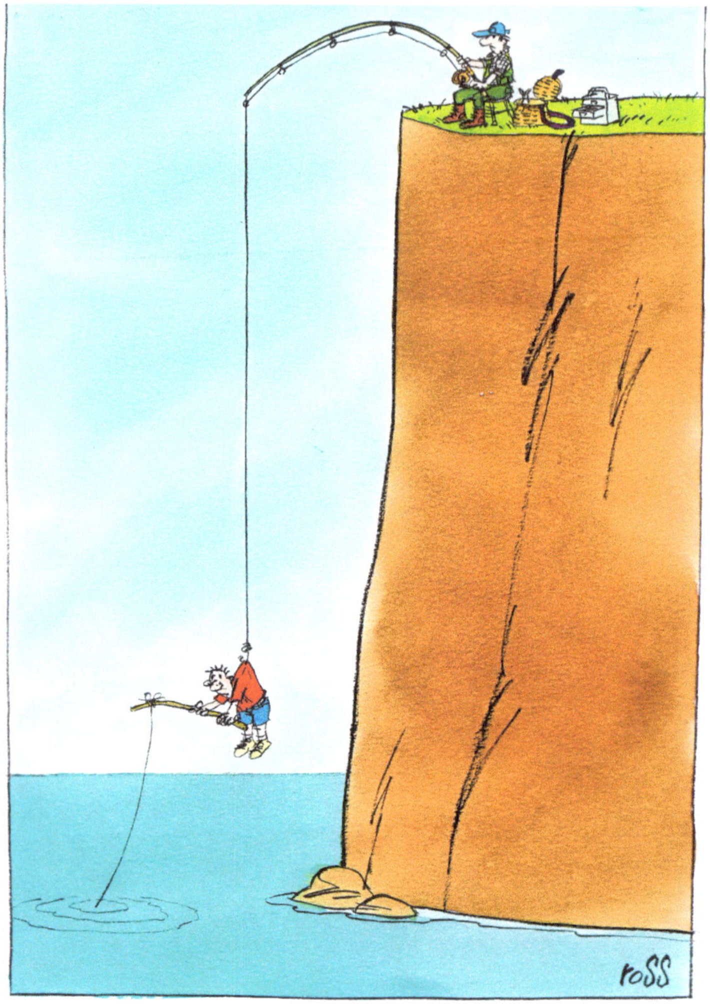
roSS

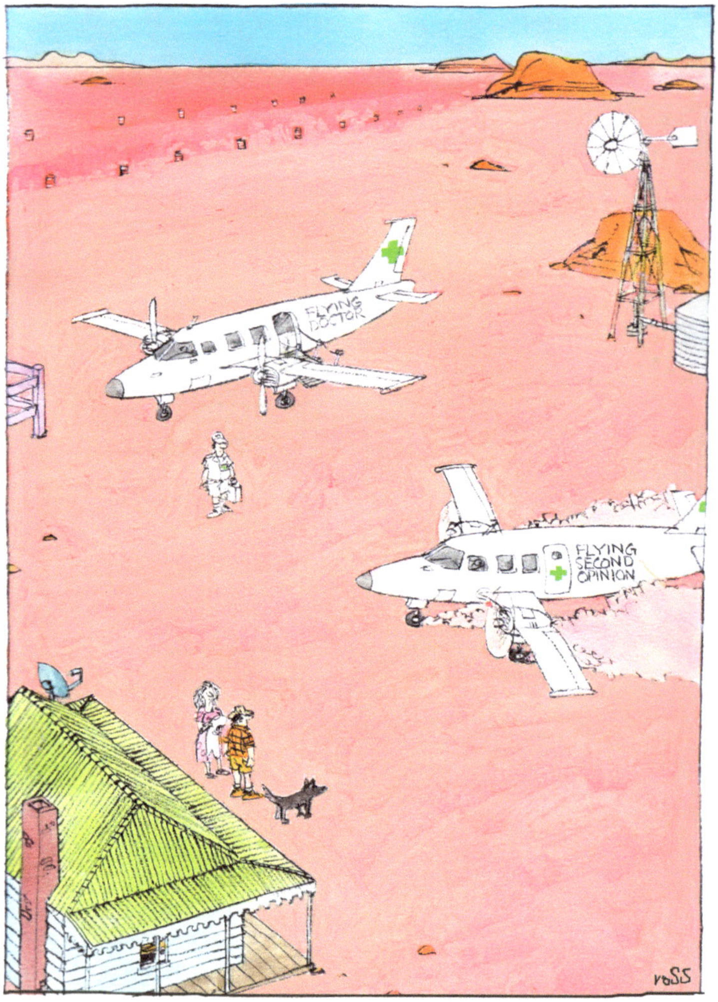
FLYING DOCTOR
FLYING SECOND OPINION
roSS

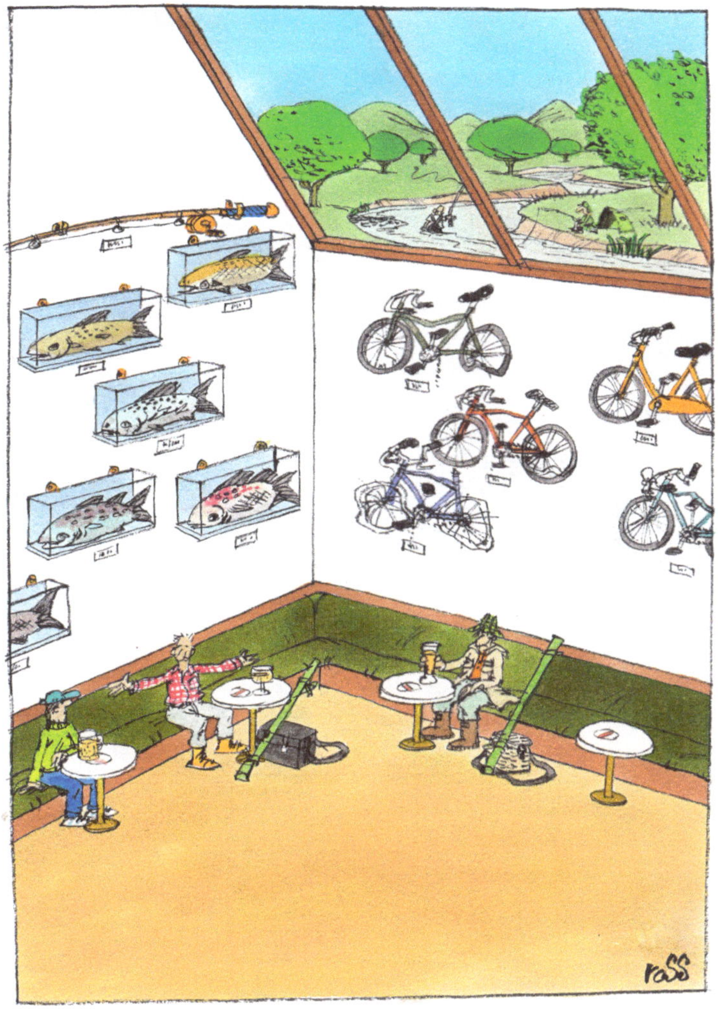
roSS

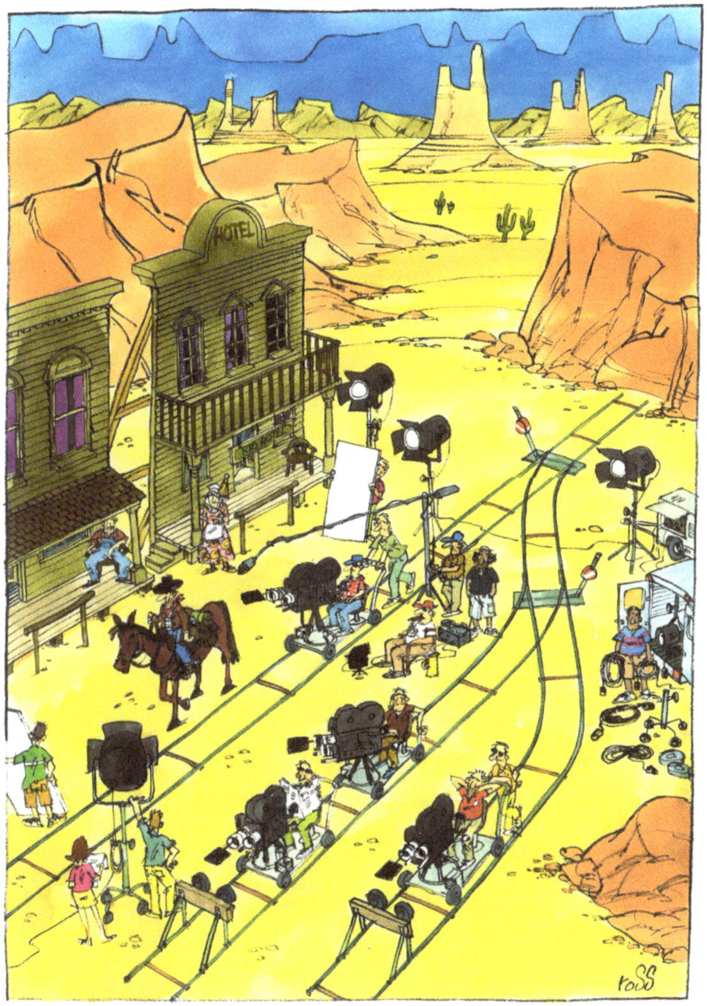
HOTEL
roSS

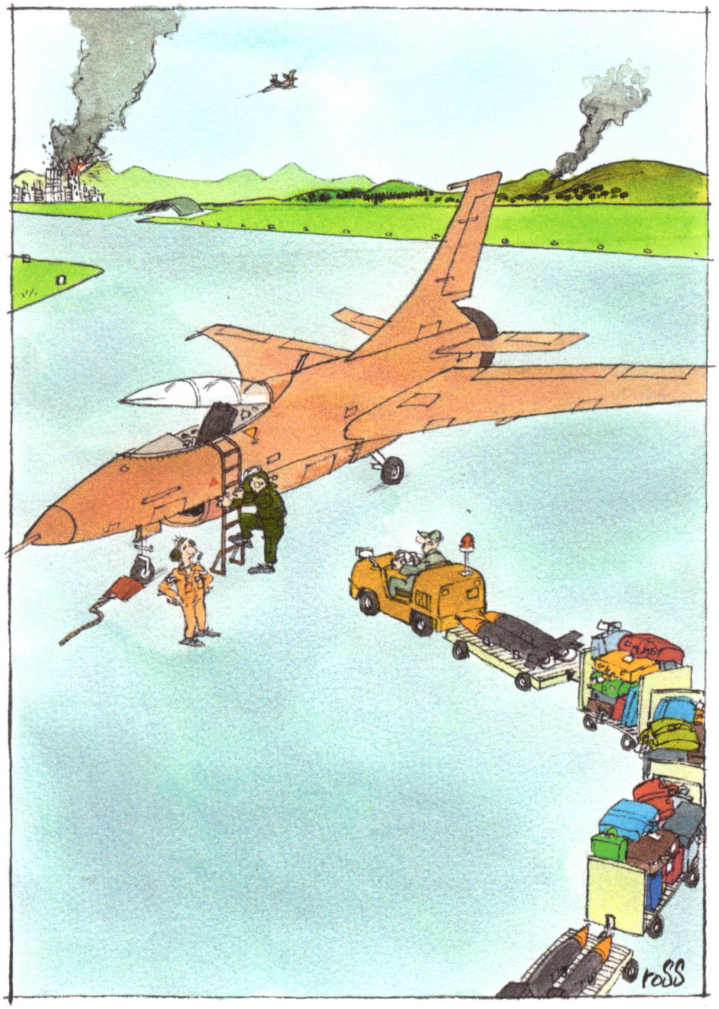
roSS

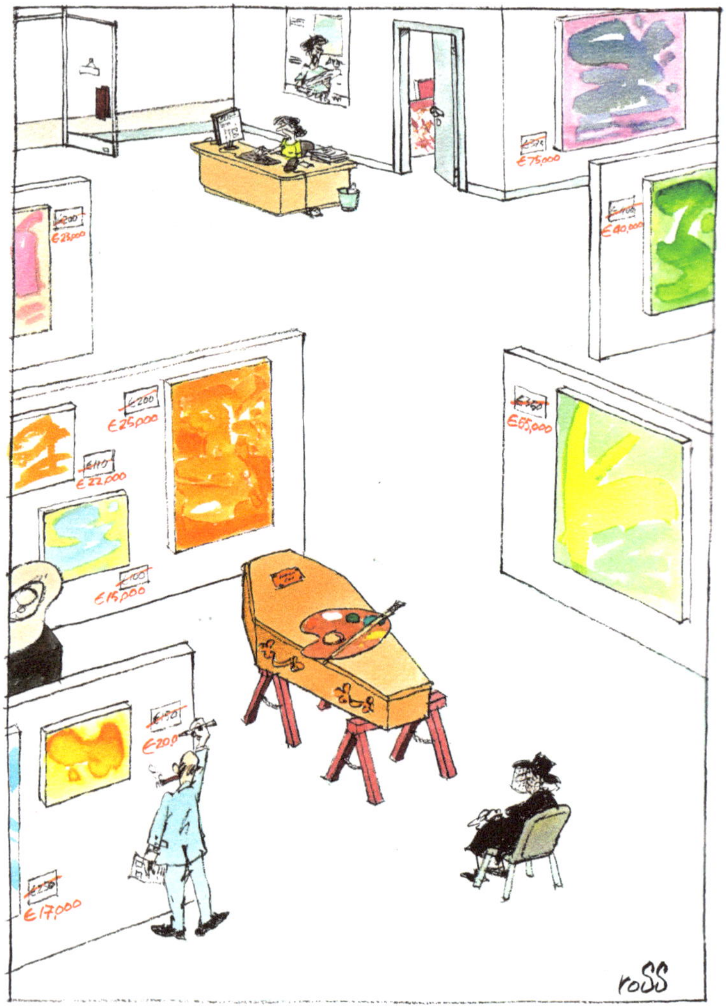
€75,000
€200
€28,000
€40,000
€200
€25,000
€350
€55,000
€110
€22,000
€100
€15,000
€150
€20,0
€250
€17,000
roSS

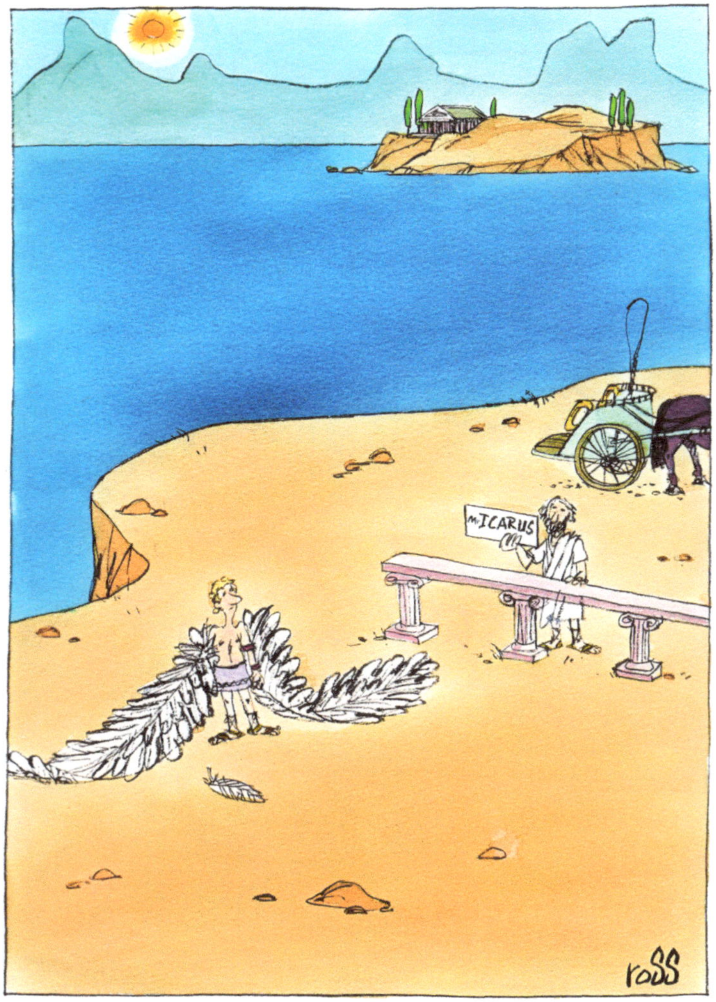

Mr ICARUS
roSS

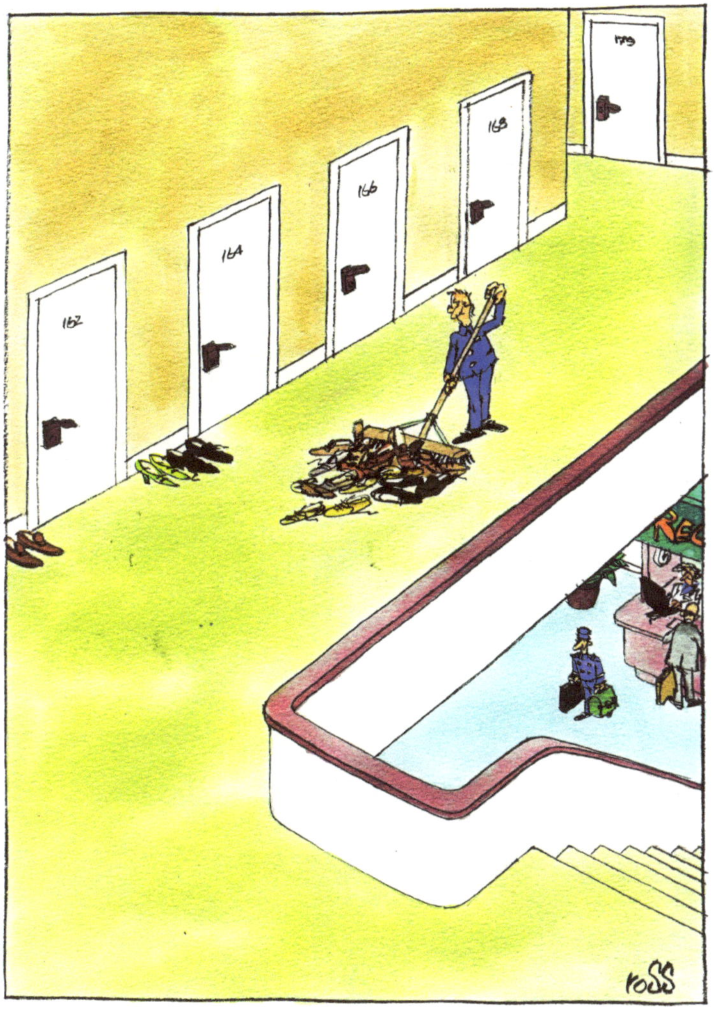

162
164
166
168
roSS

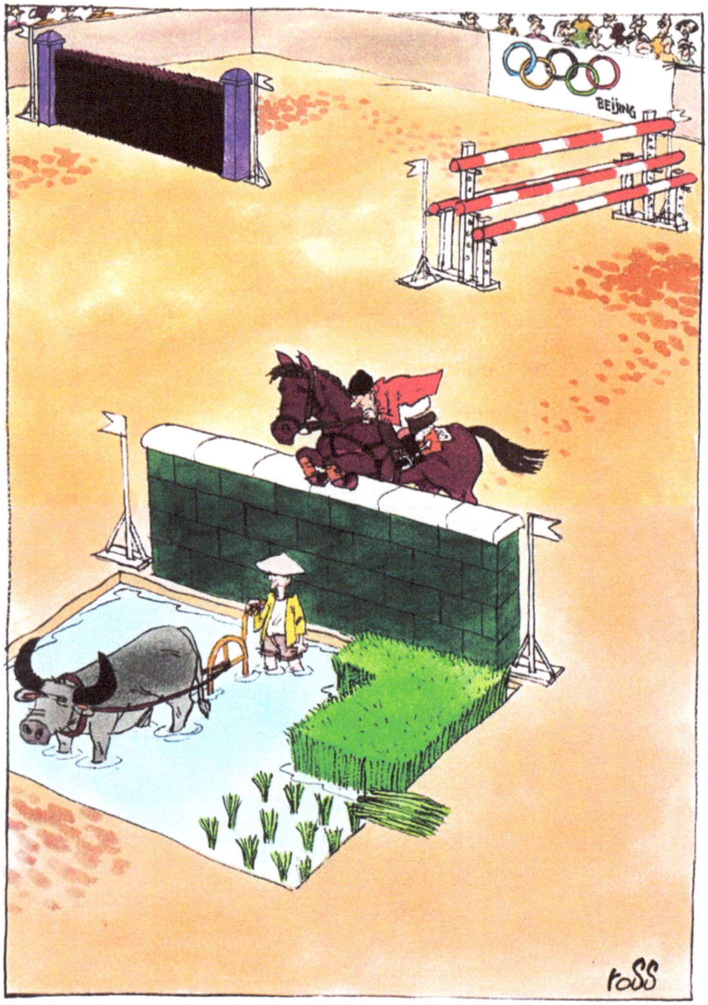

BEIJING
ross

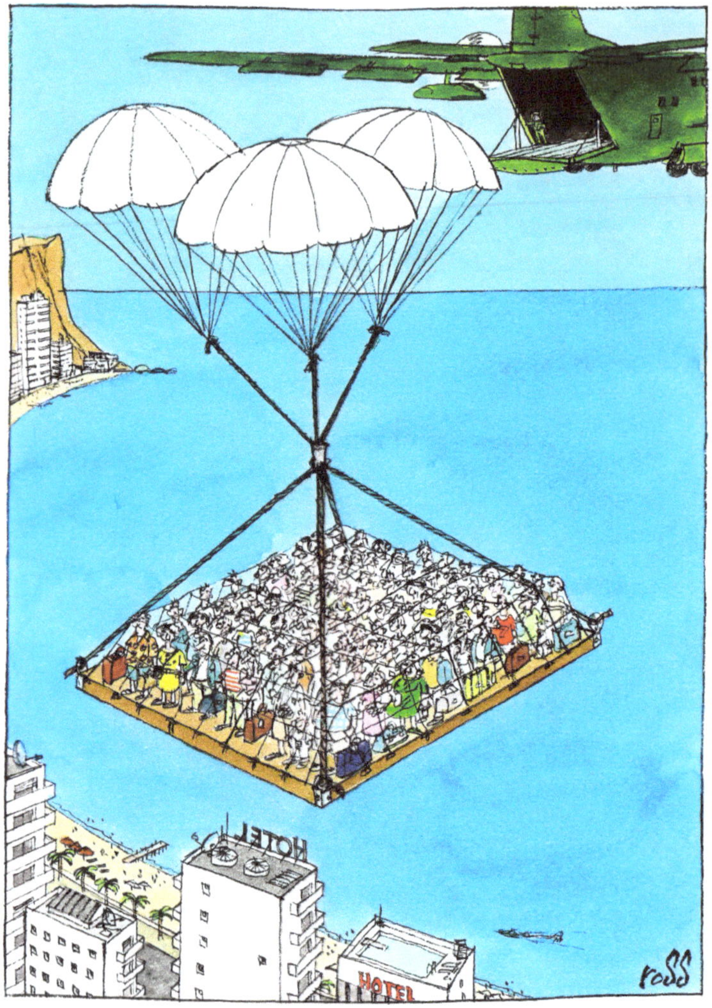

HOTEL
HOTEL
ross

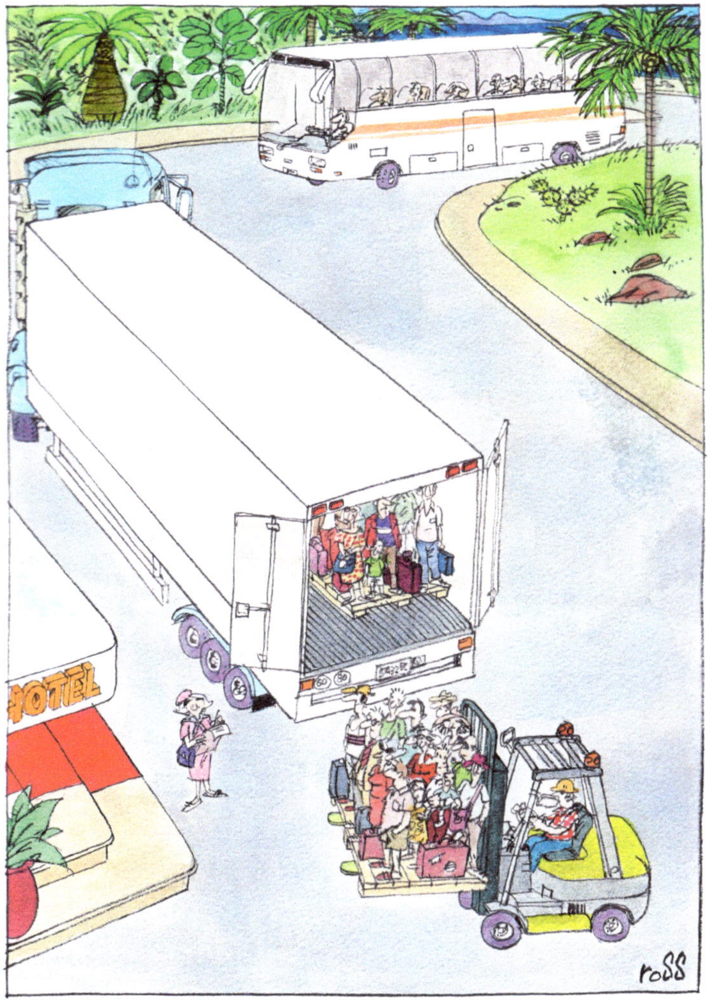
HOTEL
roSS

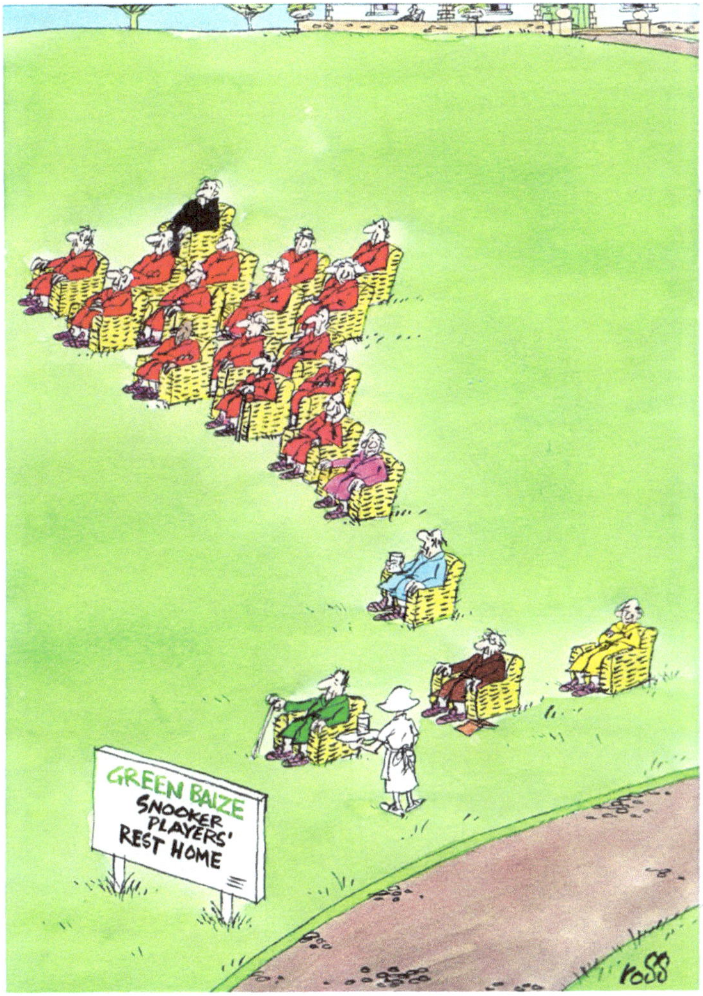
GREEN BAIZE
SNOOKER
PLAYERS'
REST HOME
roSS

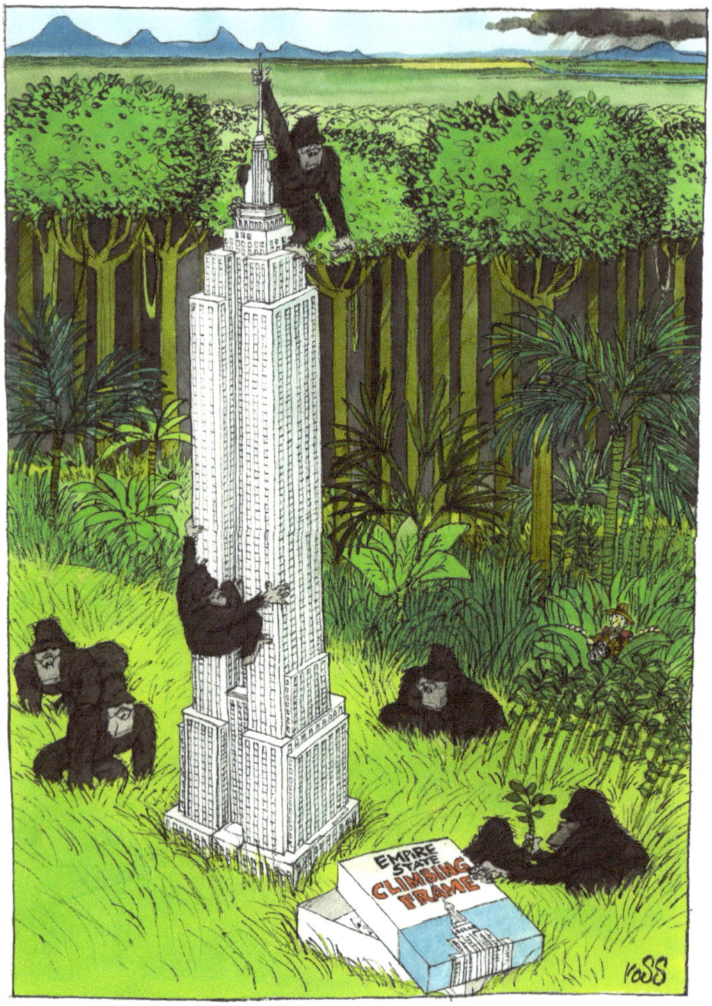
EMPIRE STATE
CLIMBING FRAME
roSS

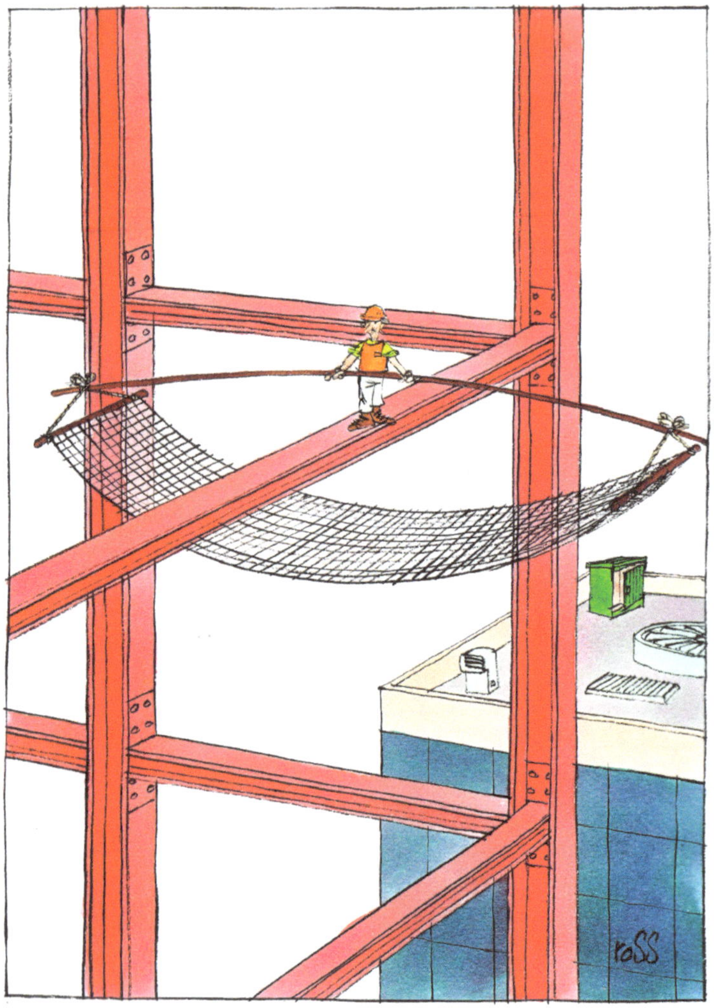
roSS

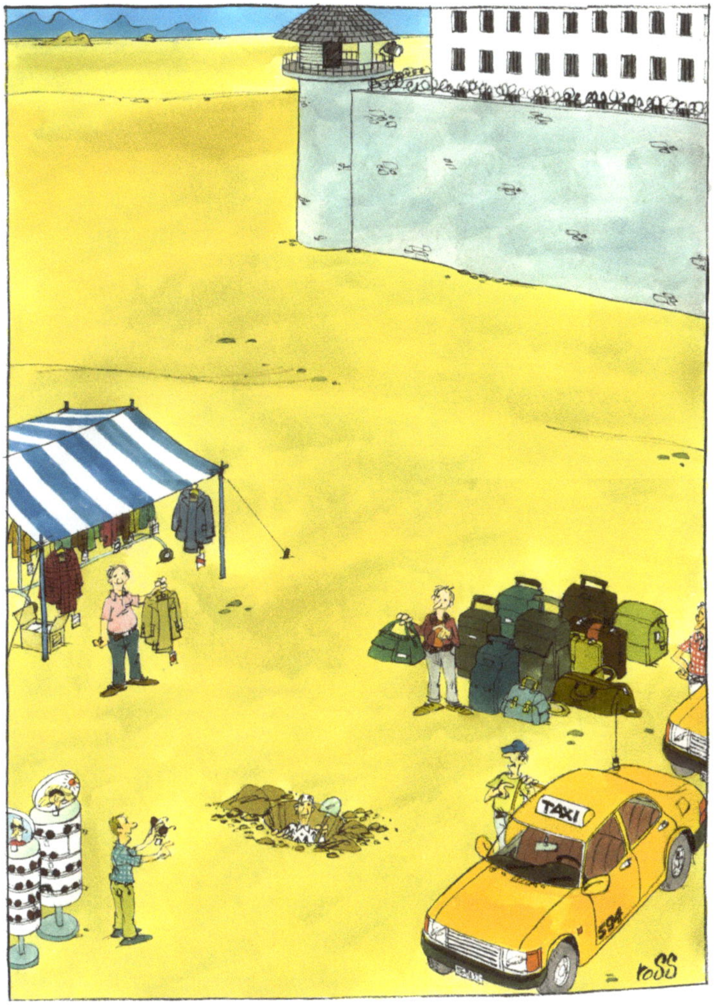
TAXI
594
roSS

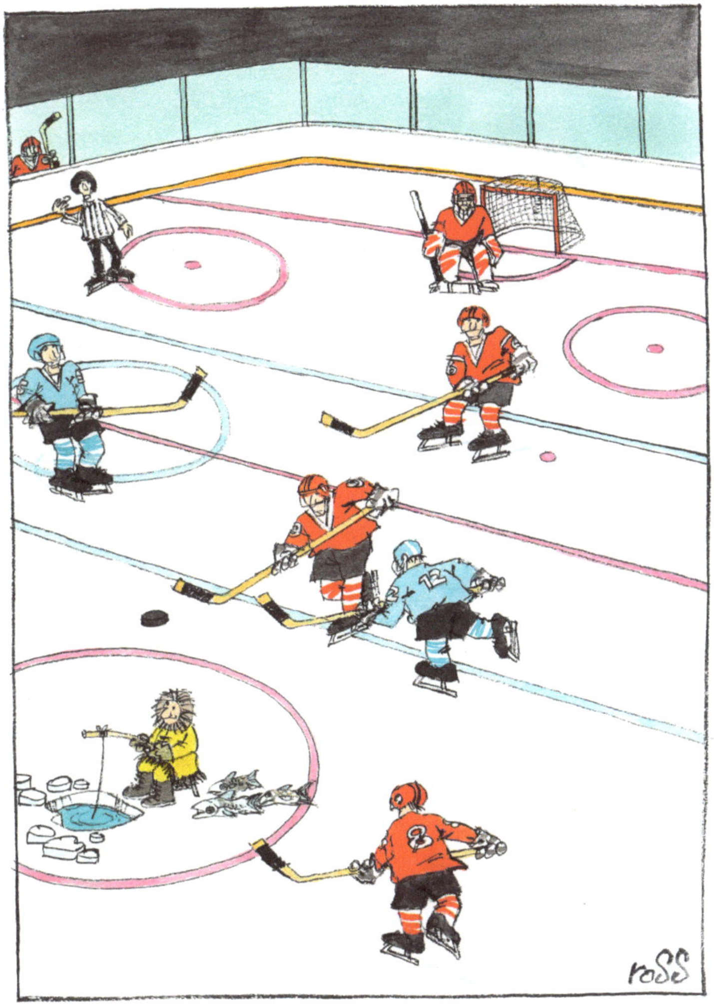
12
8
roSS

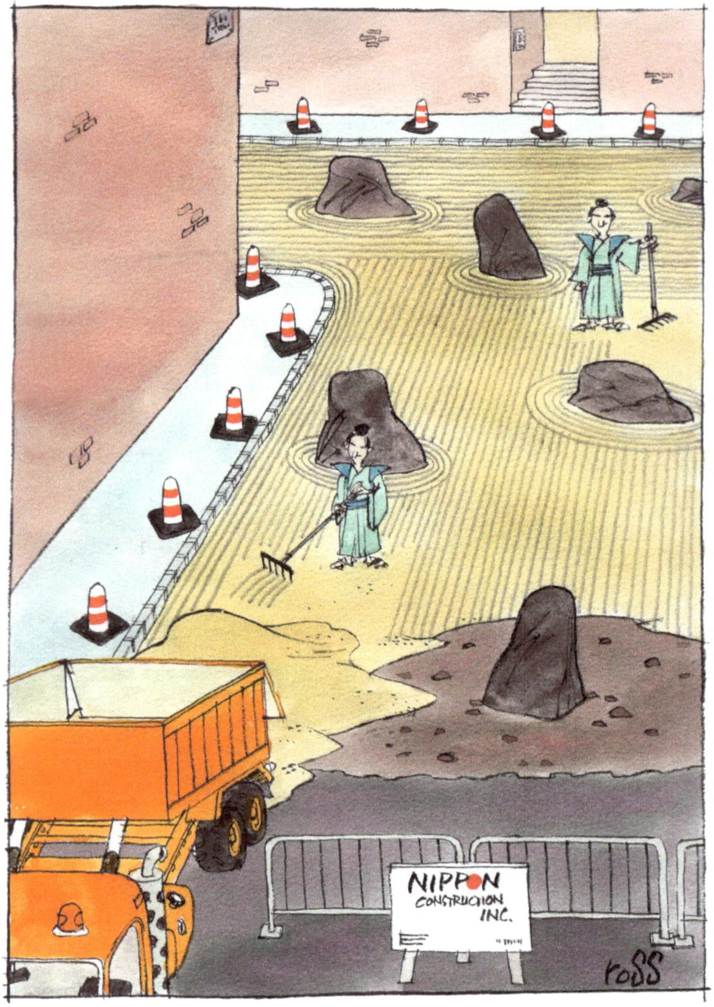
NIPPON
CONSTRUCTION
INC.
roSS

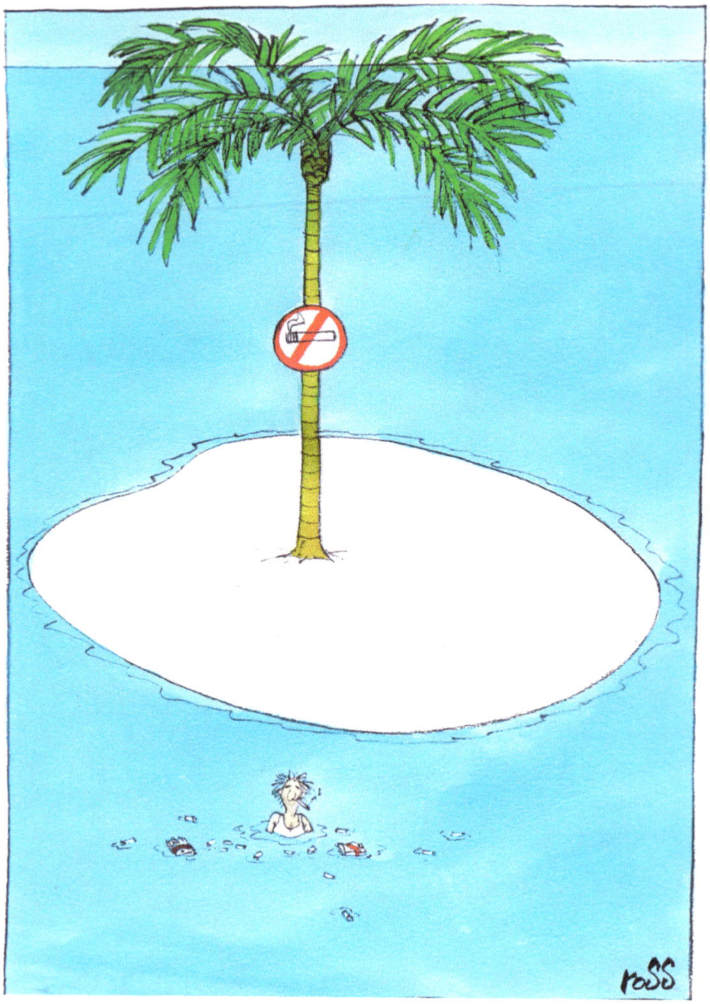
roSS

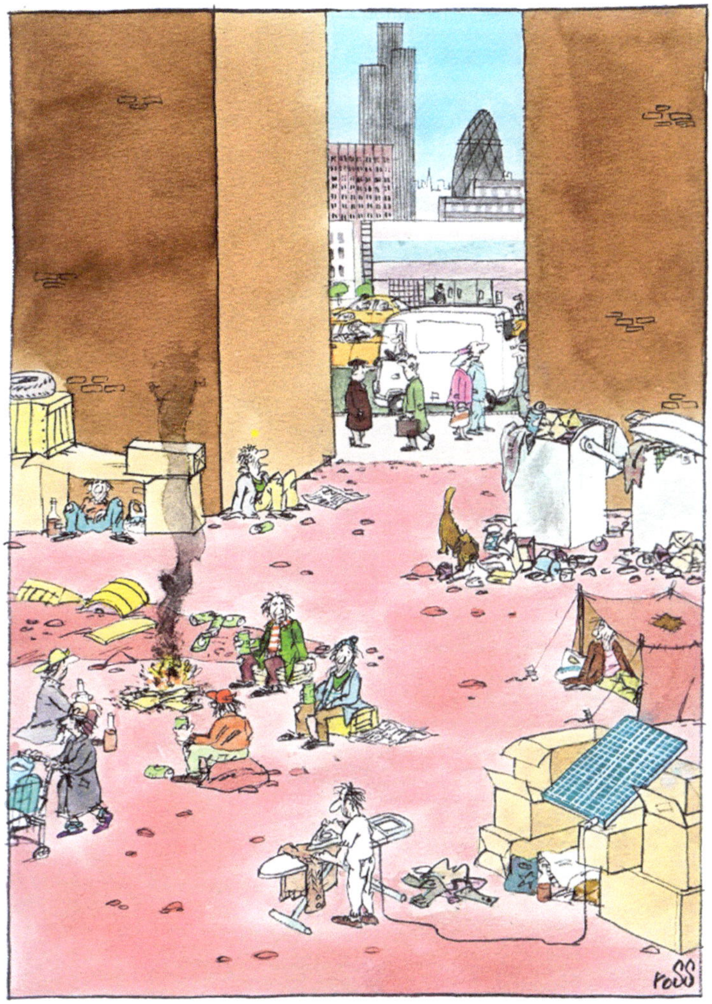
ross

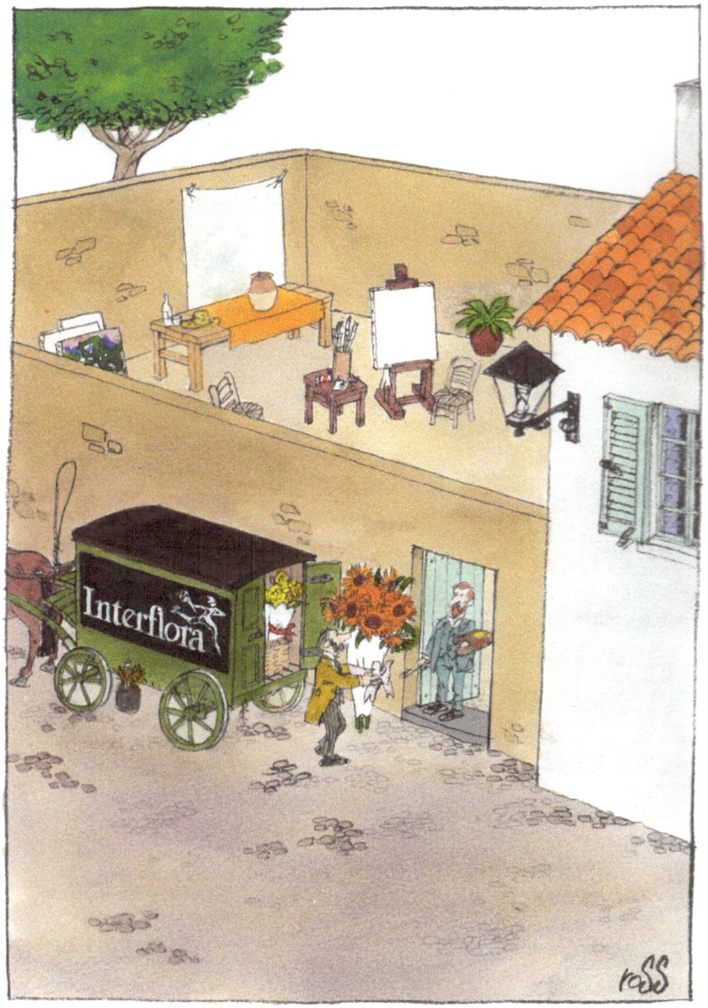
Interflora
ross

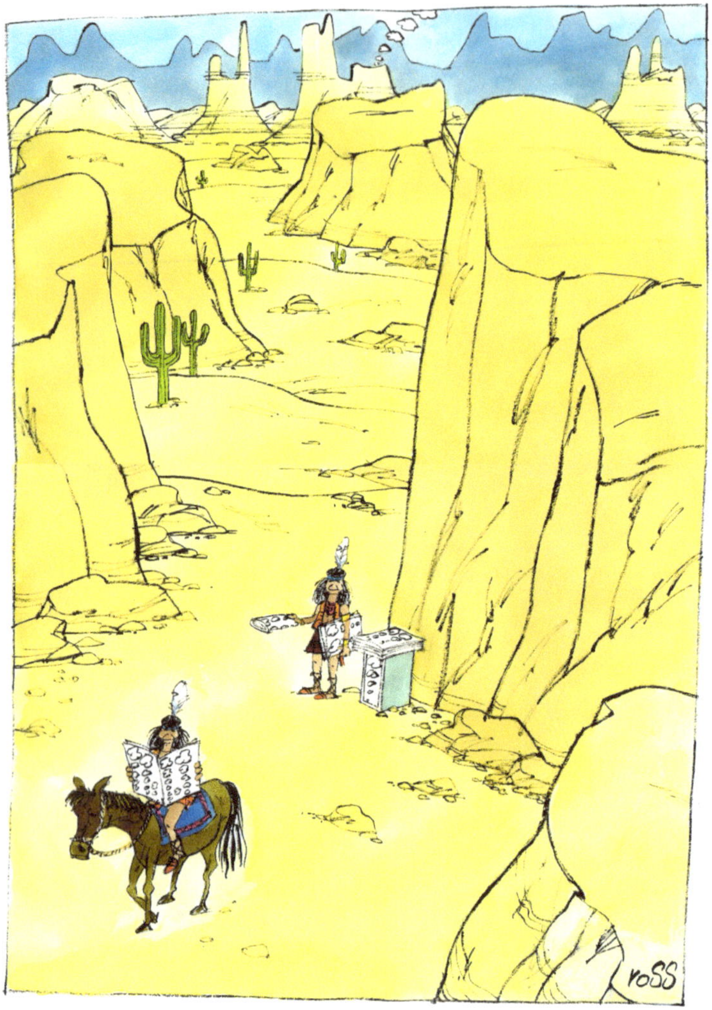
roSS

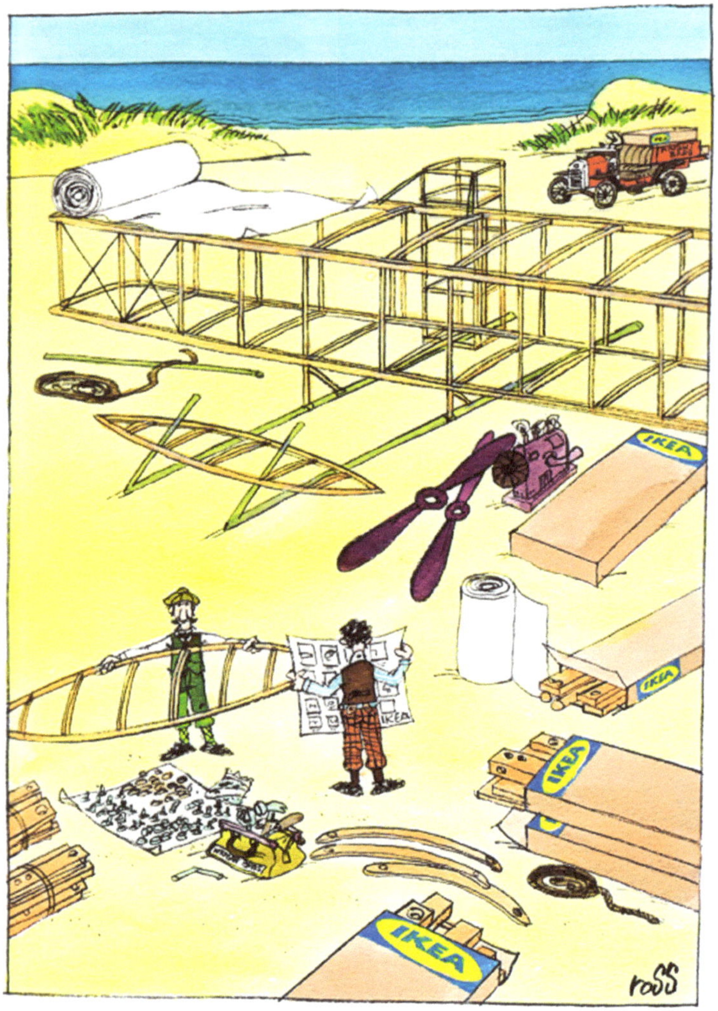
IKEA
IKEA
IKEA
IKEA
roSS

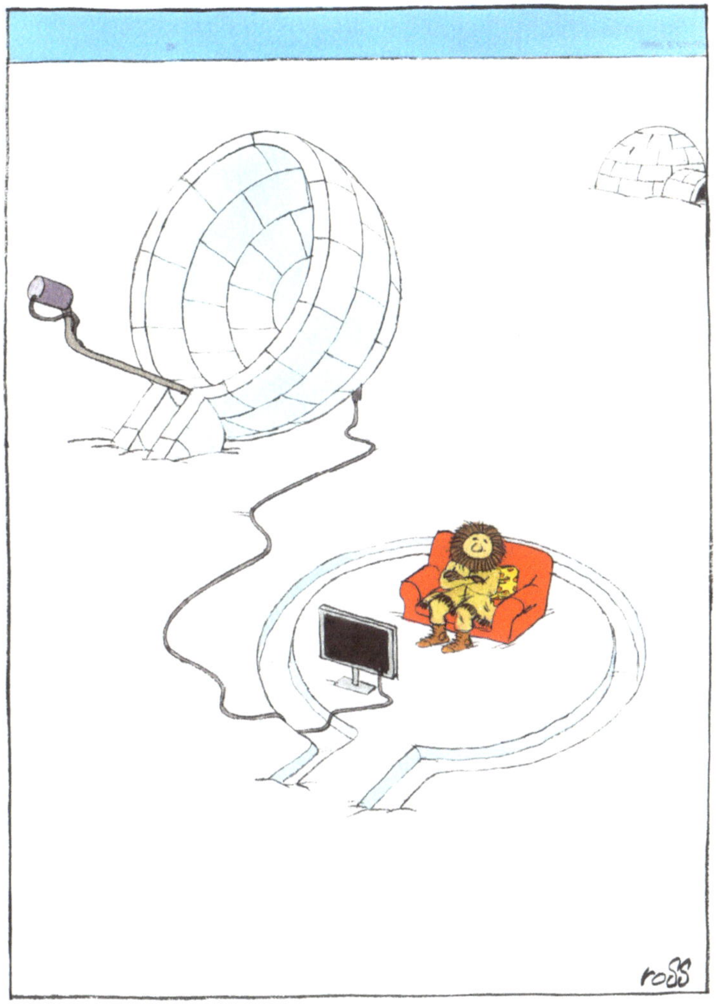
roSS

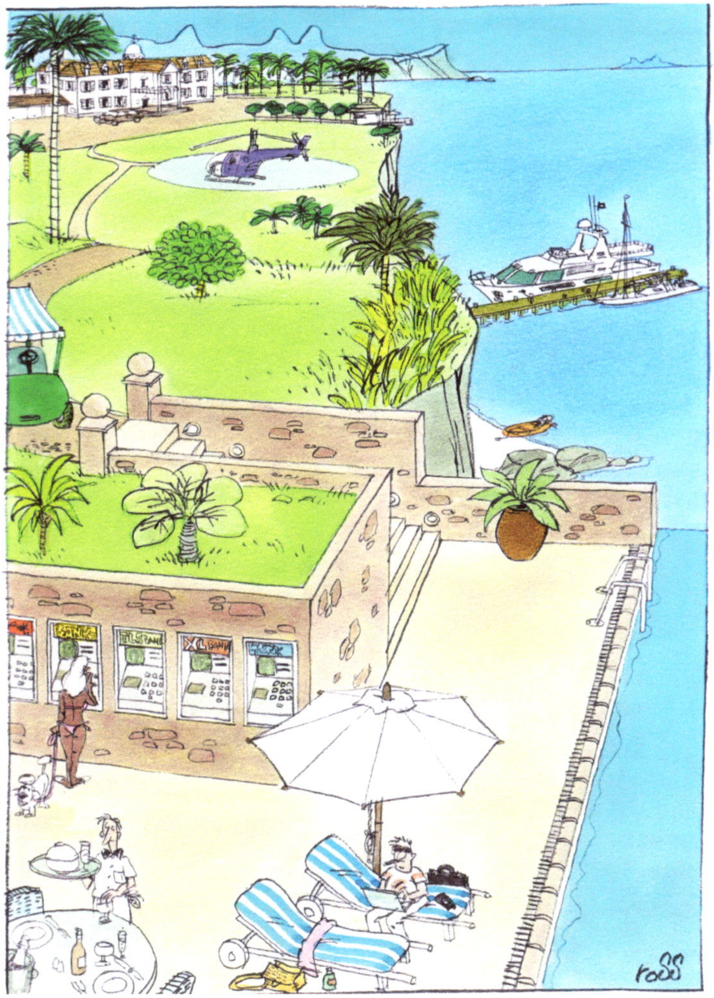
XL BANK
roSS

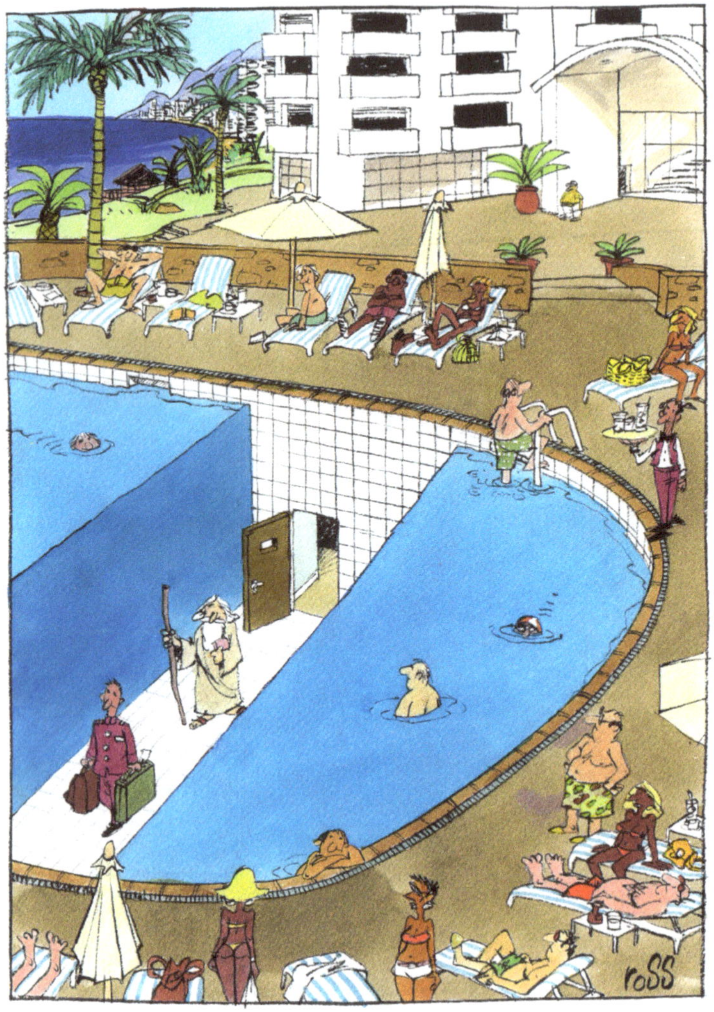
roSS

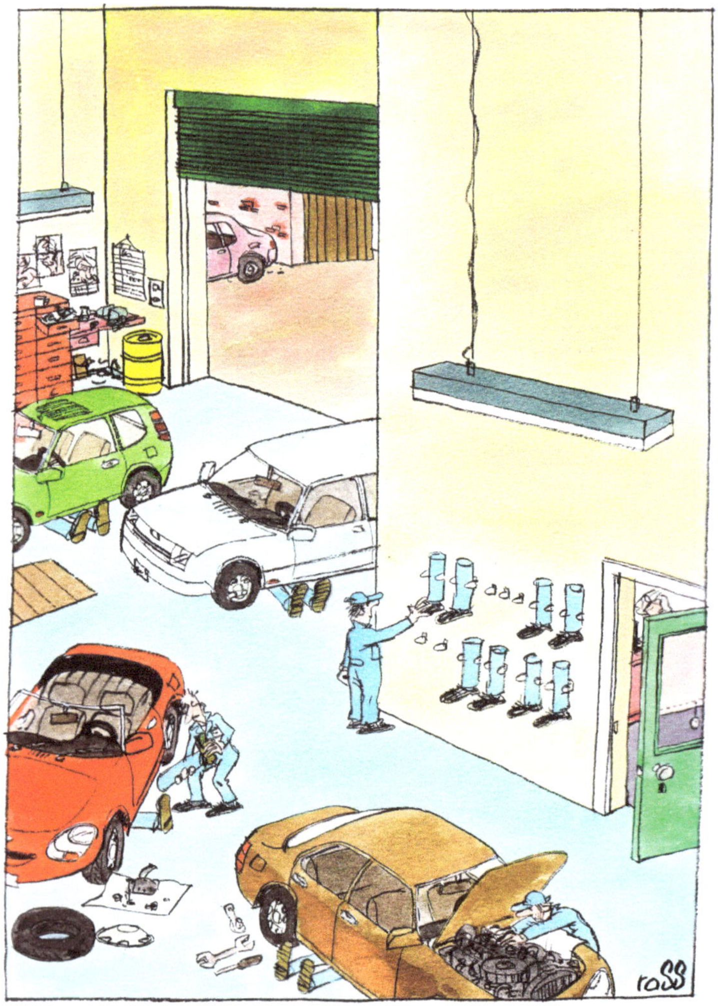
roSS

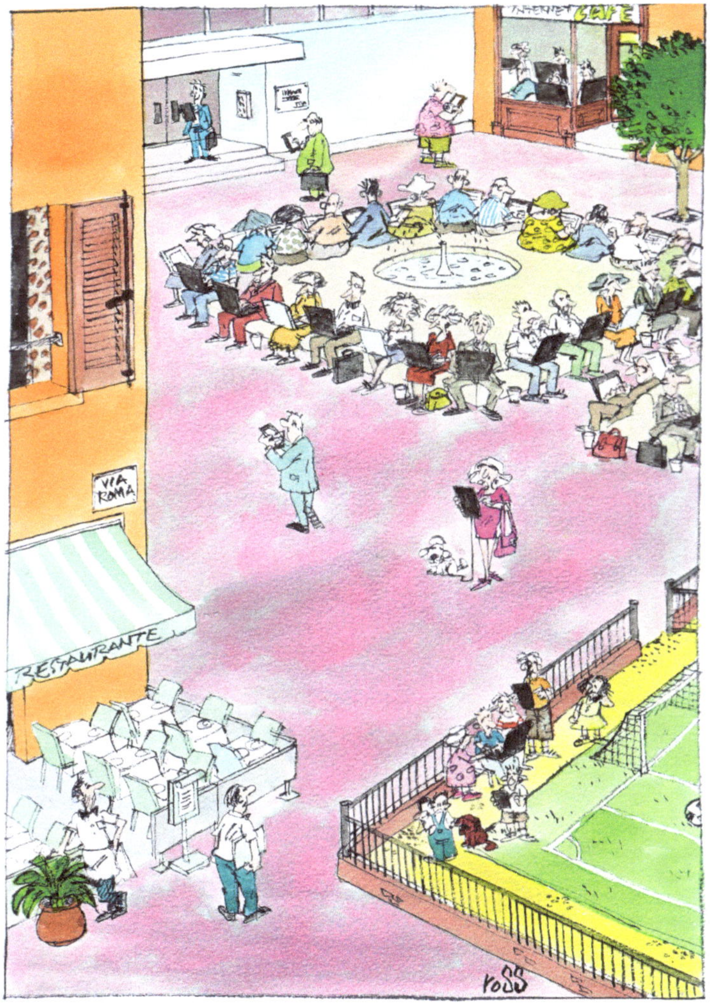
INTERNET CAFE
VIA ROMA
RESTAURANTE
ross

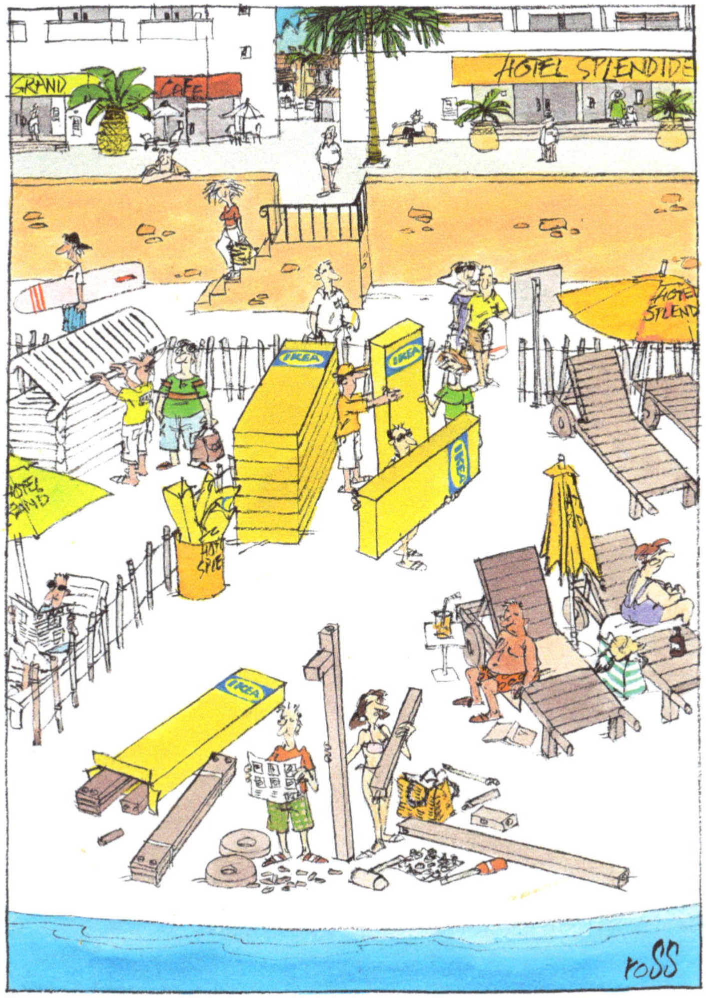
GRAND
CAFE
HOTEL SPLENDIDE
IKEA
IKEA
IKEA
IKEA
HOTEL SPLEND
HOTEL GRAND
ross

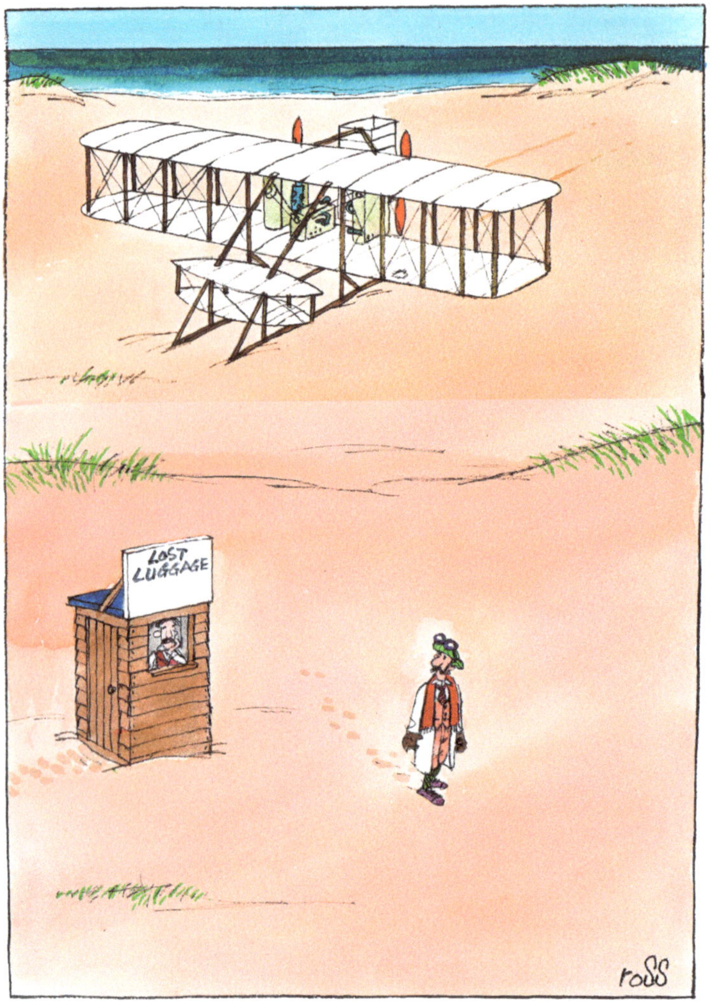
LOST LUGGAGE
ross

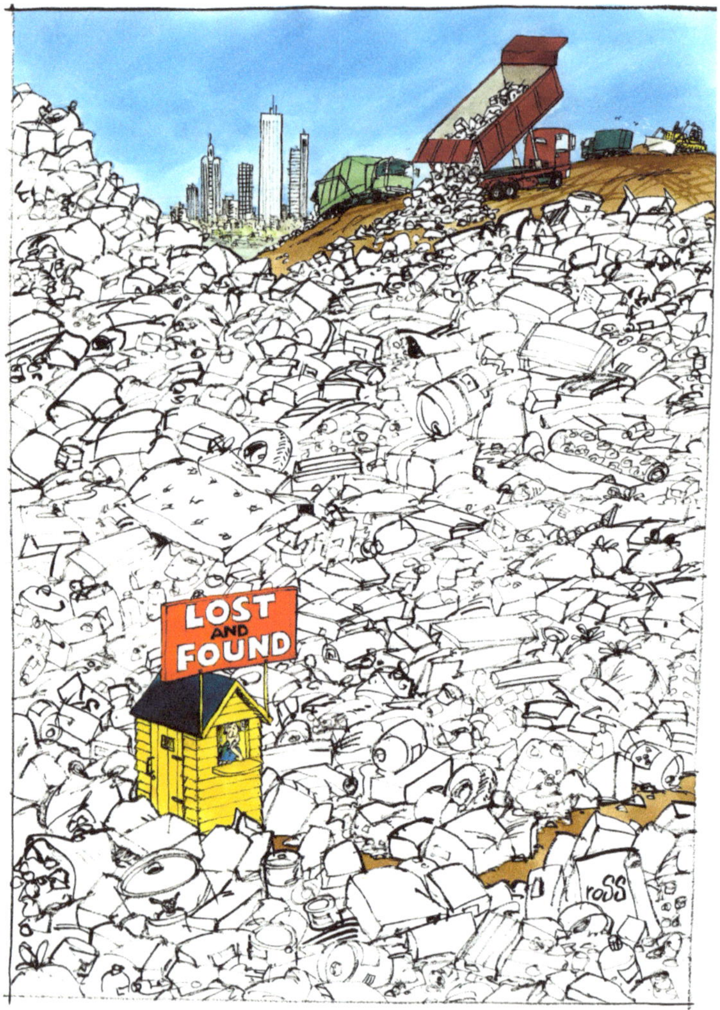
LOST AND FOUND
ross

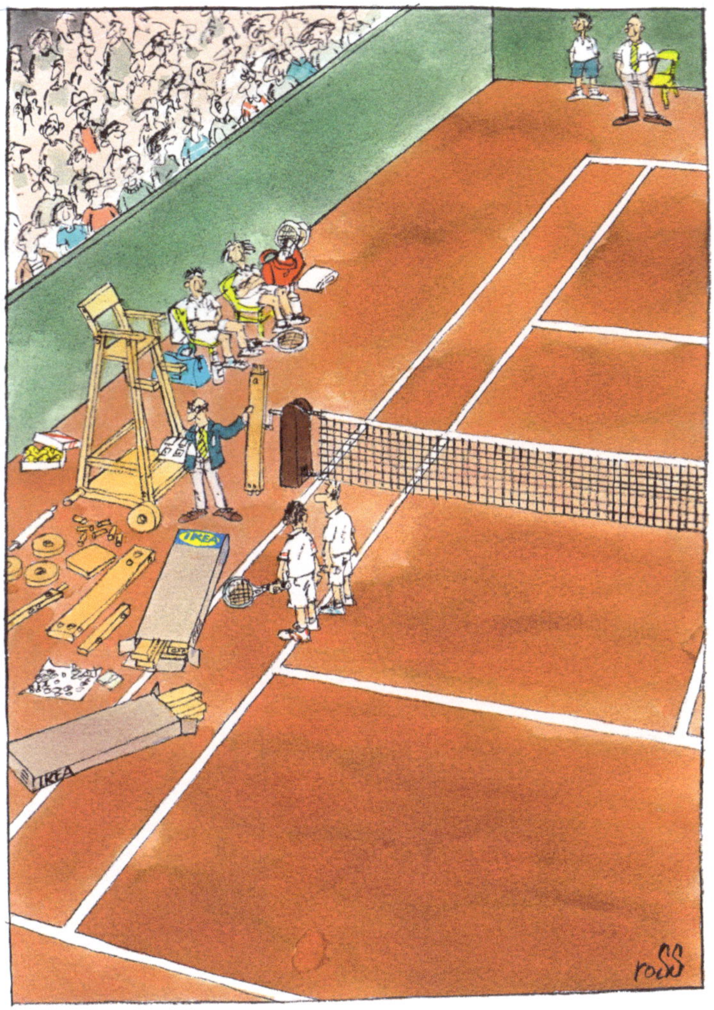
IKEA
IKEA
roSS

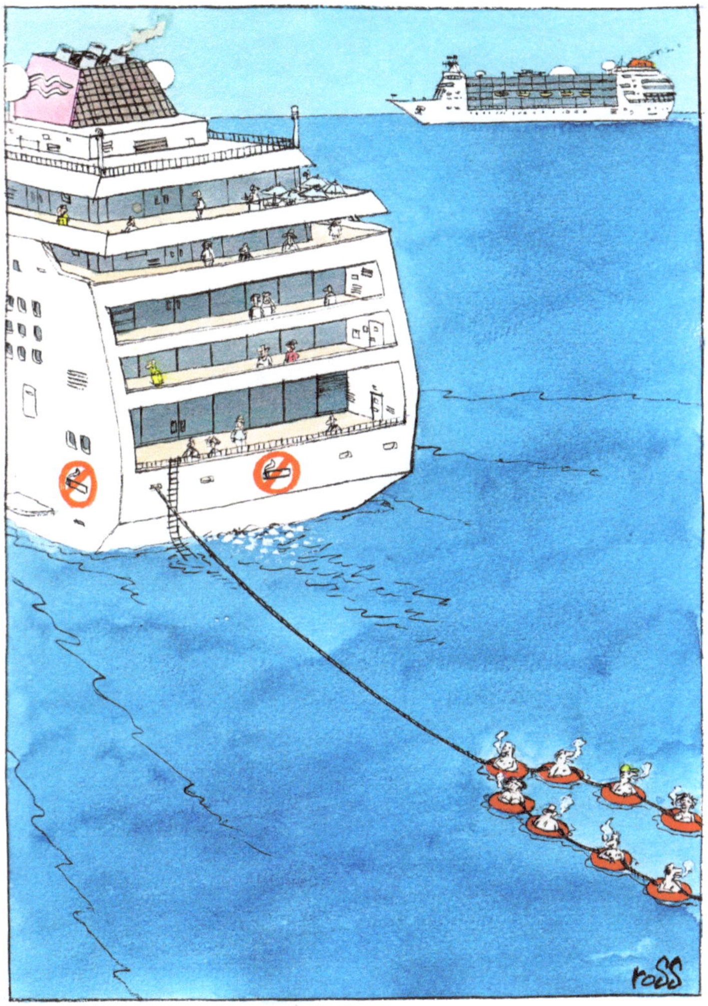
roSS

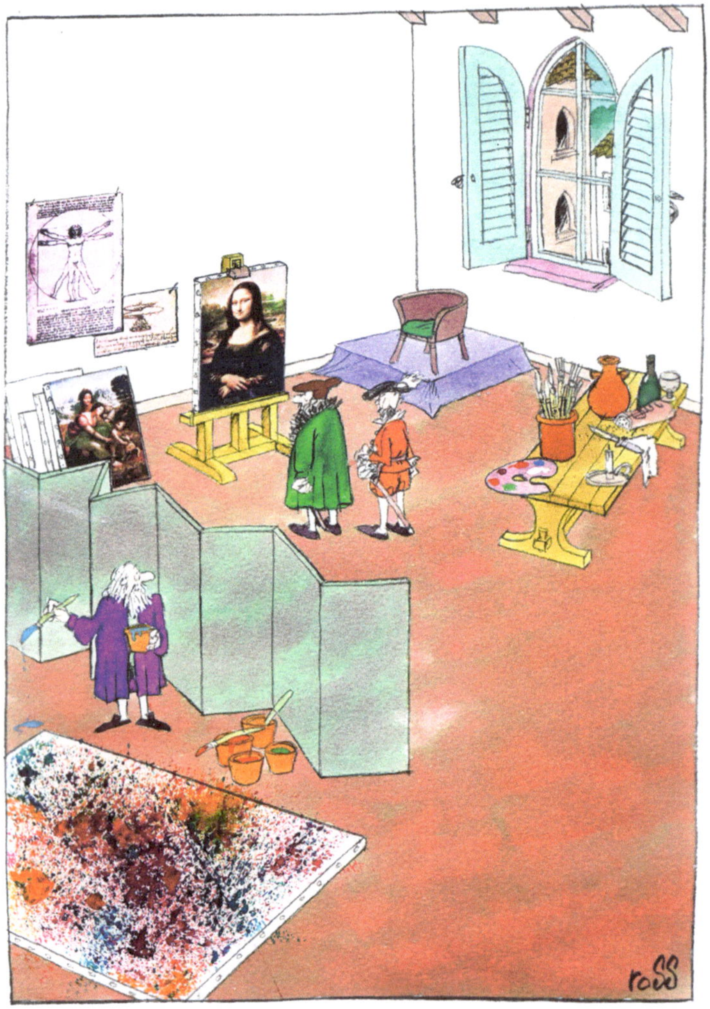
roSS

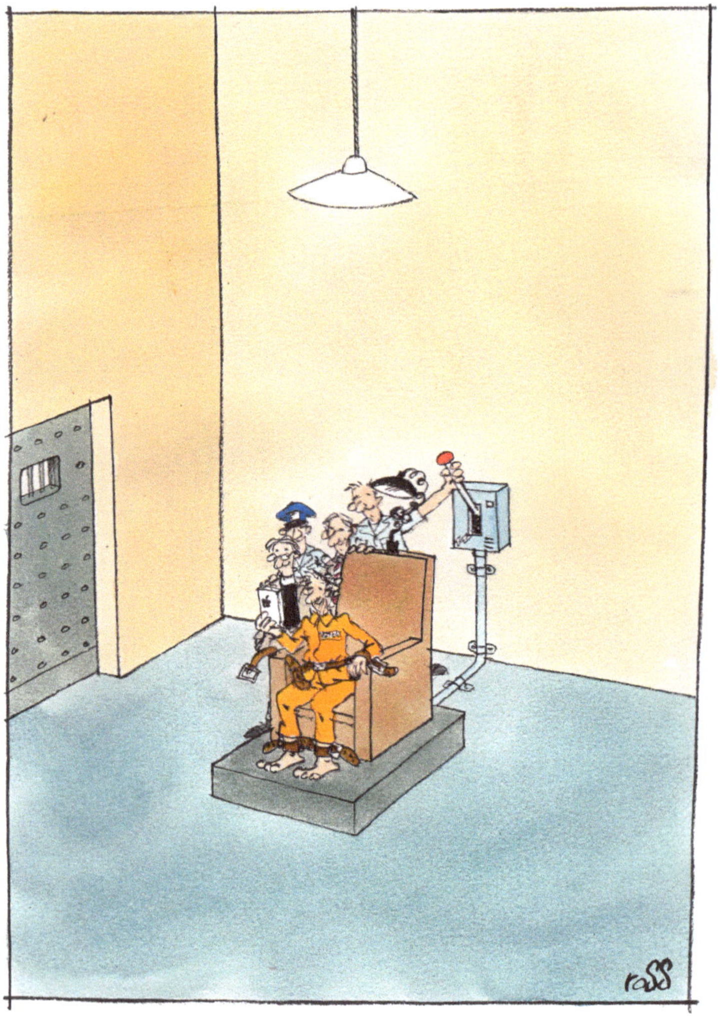
roSS

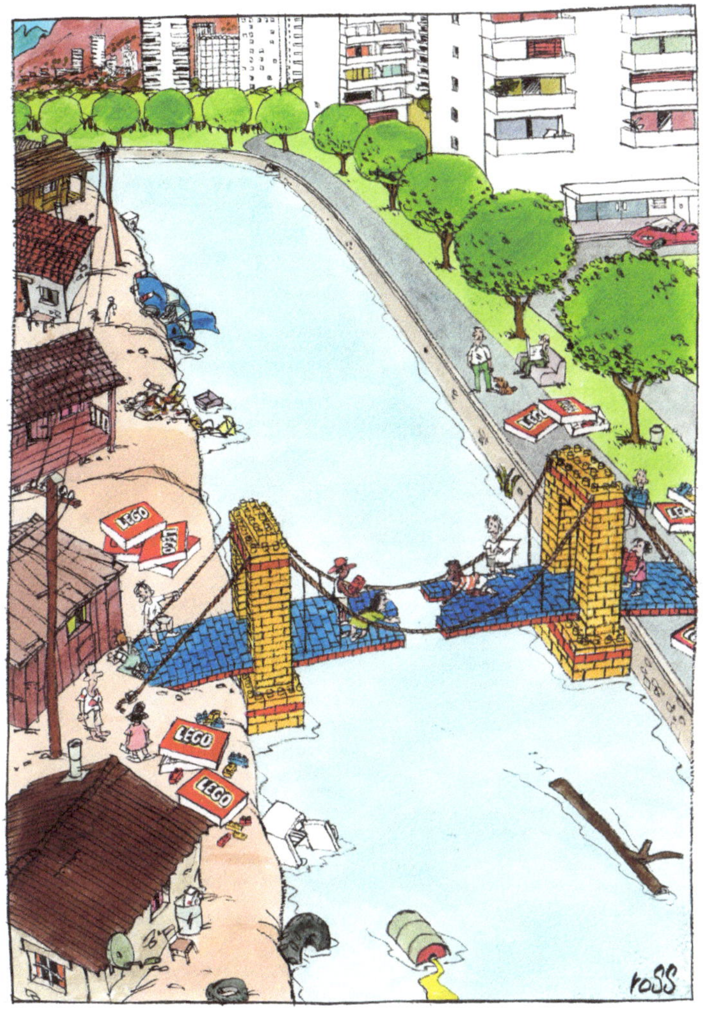
LEGO
LEGO
LEGO
LEGO
roSS

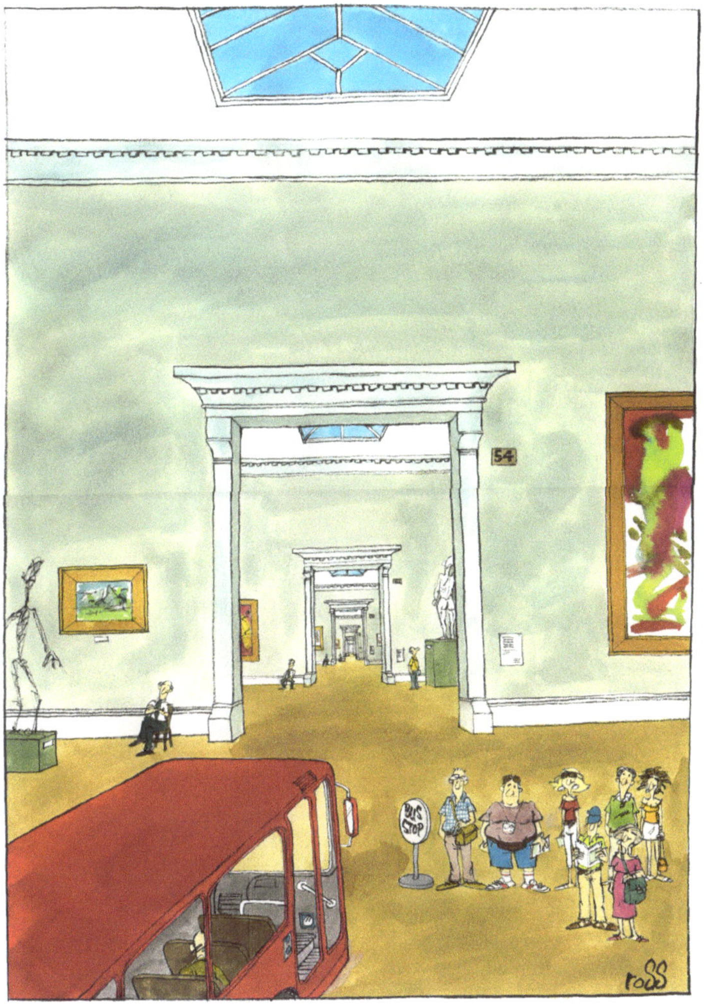
54
BUS STOP
roSS

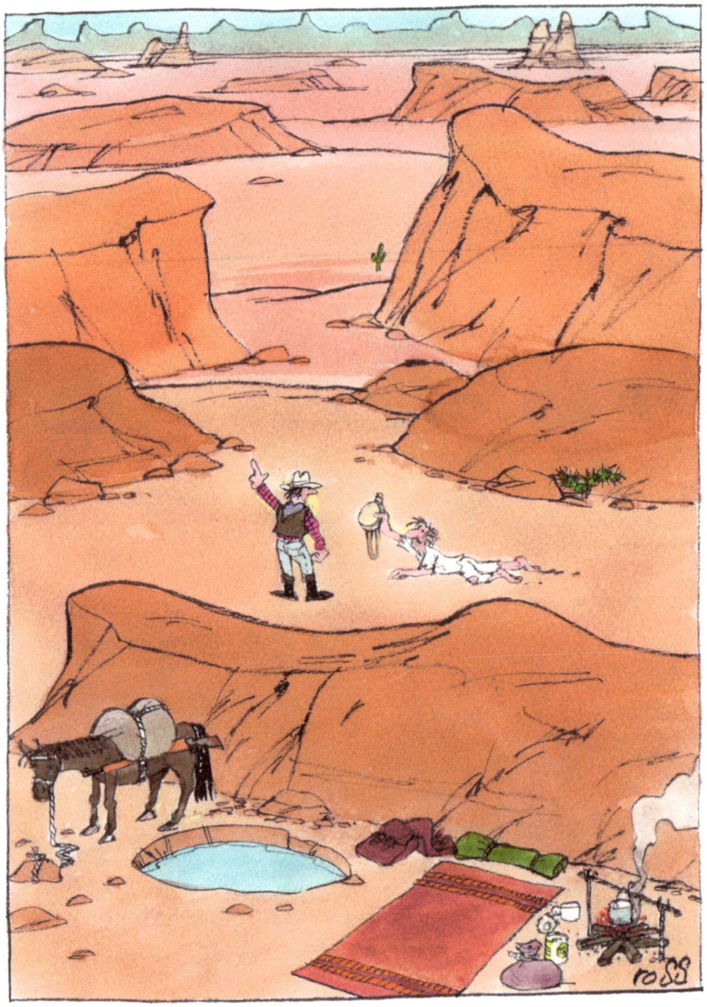
roSS

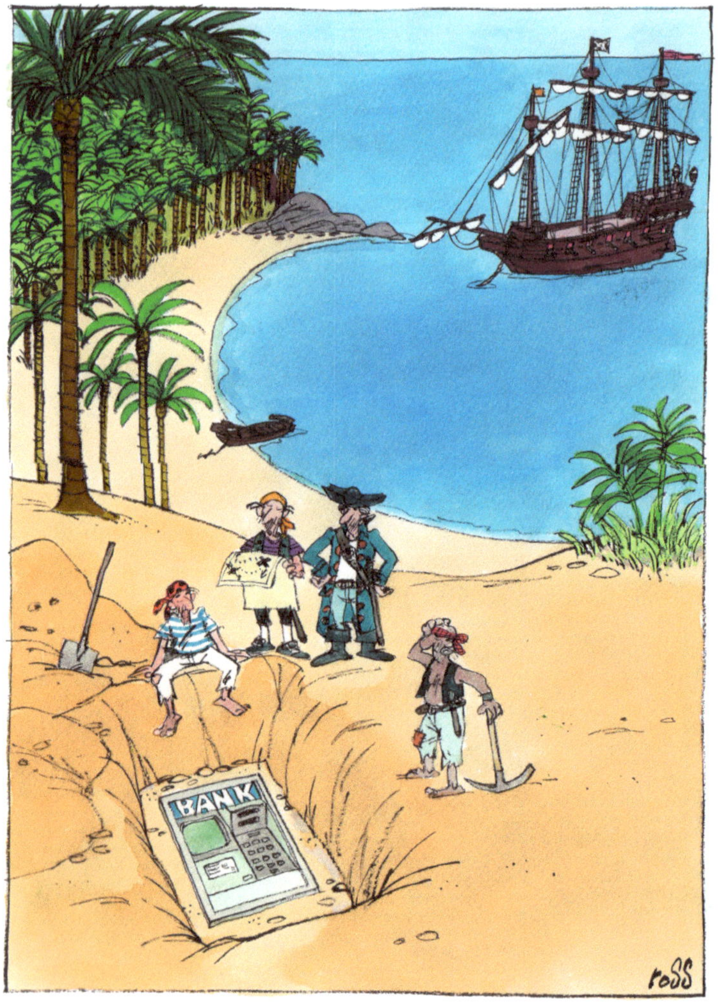
BANK
roSS

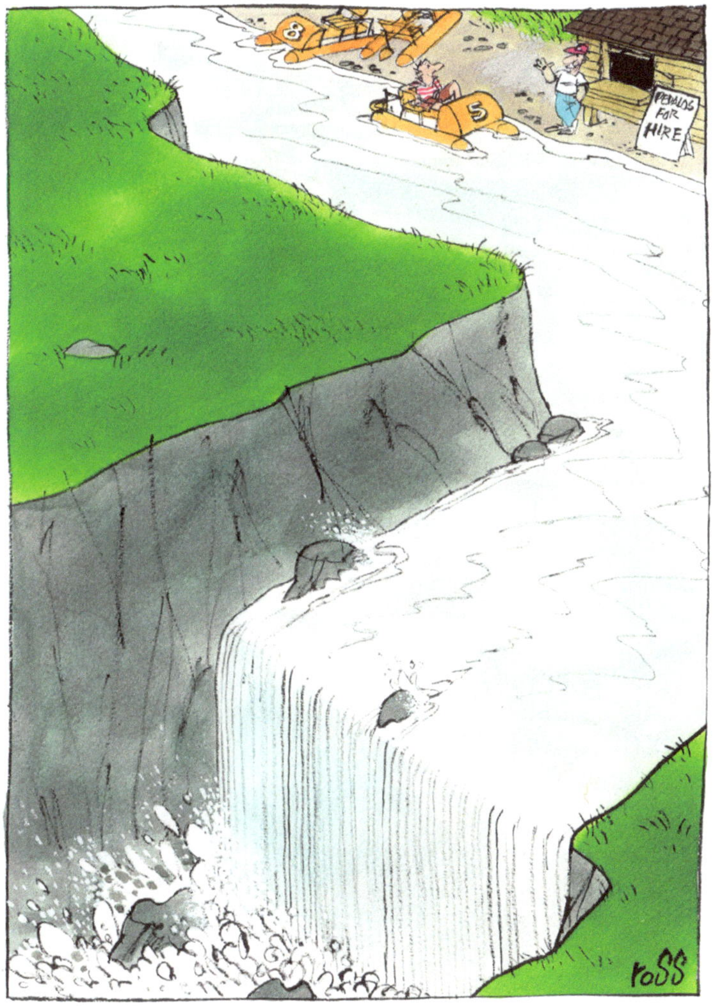
PEDALOS FOR HIRE
roSS

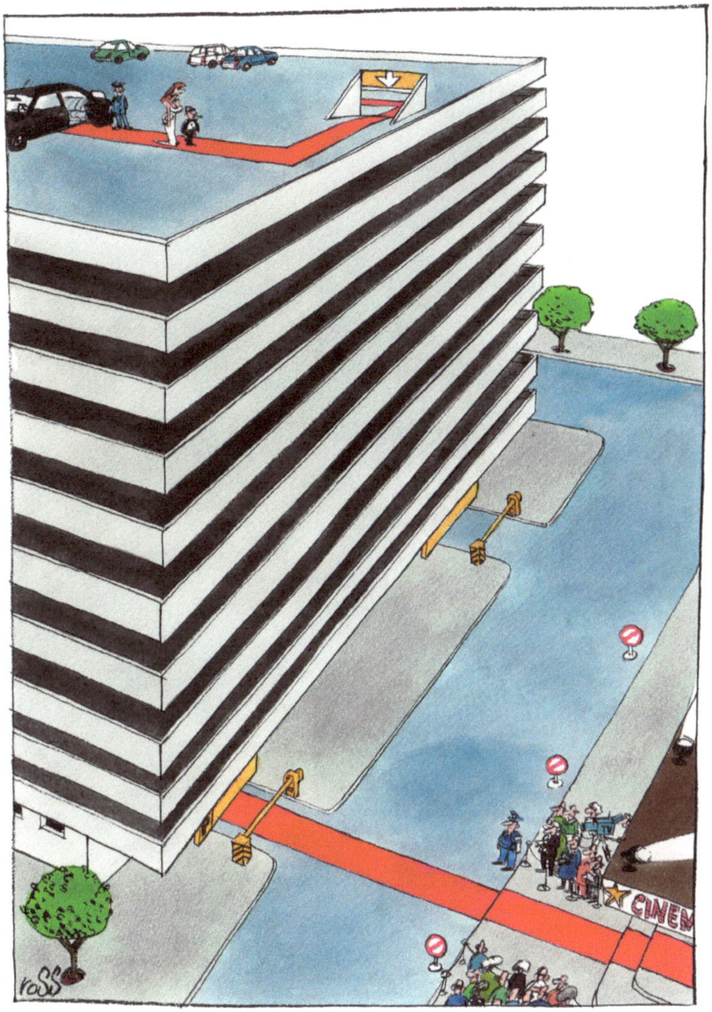
CINEM
roSS

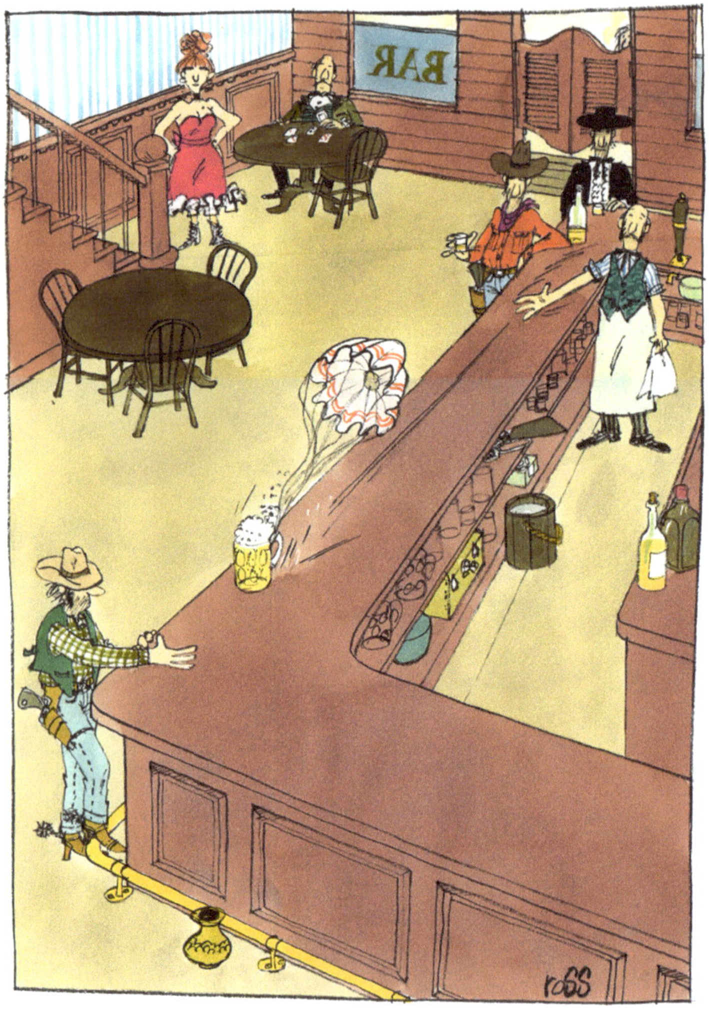
BAR
roSS

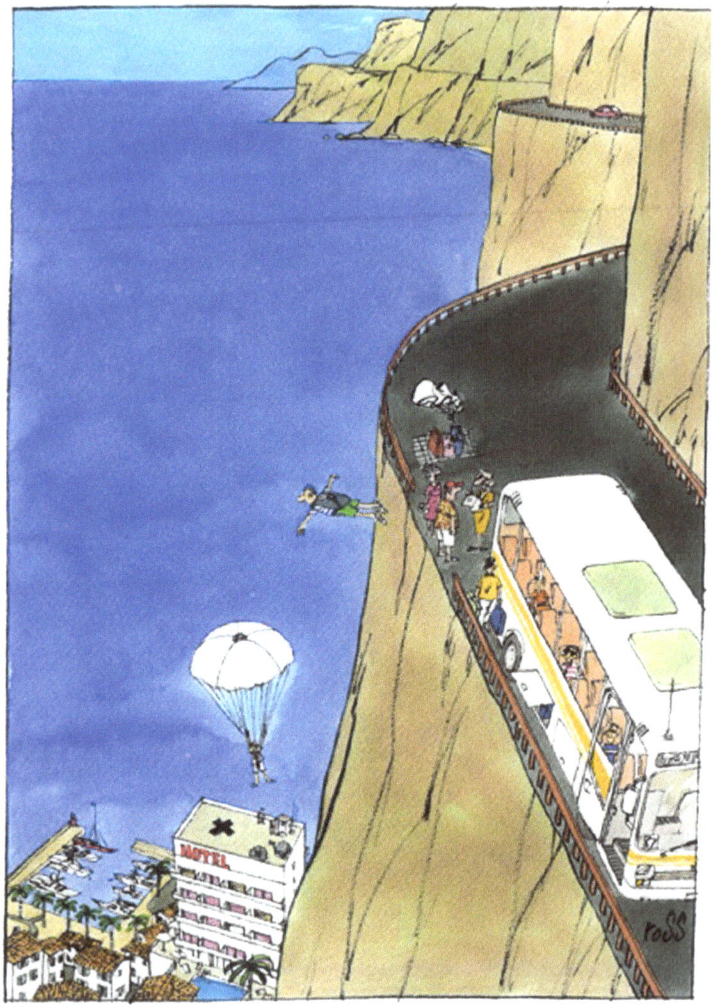
HOTEL
roSS

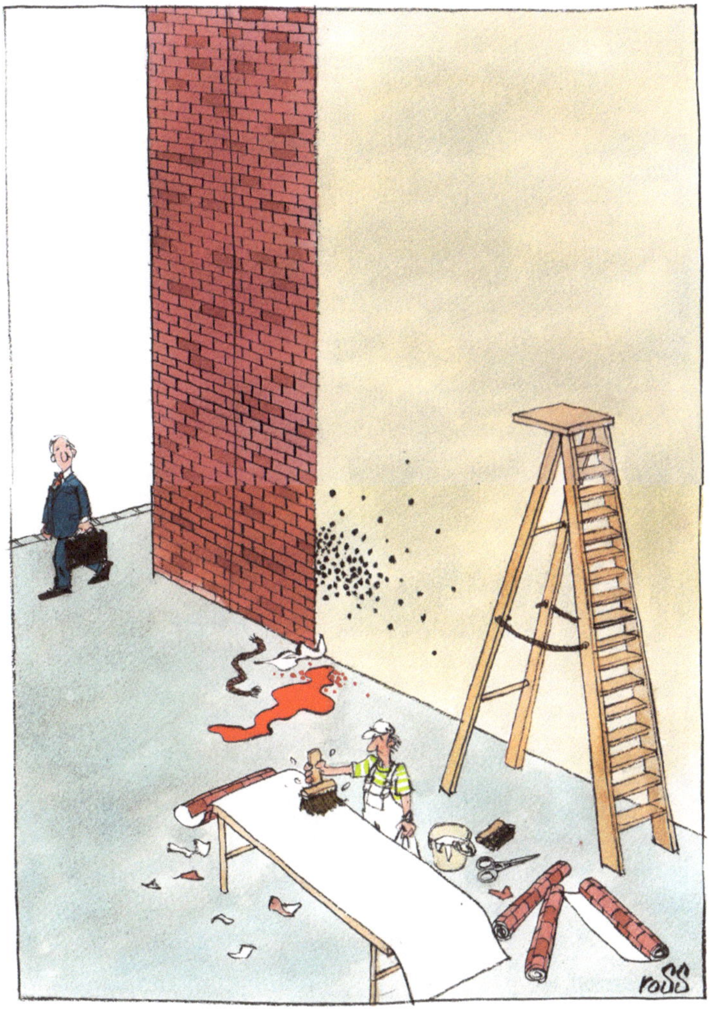
roSS

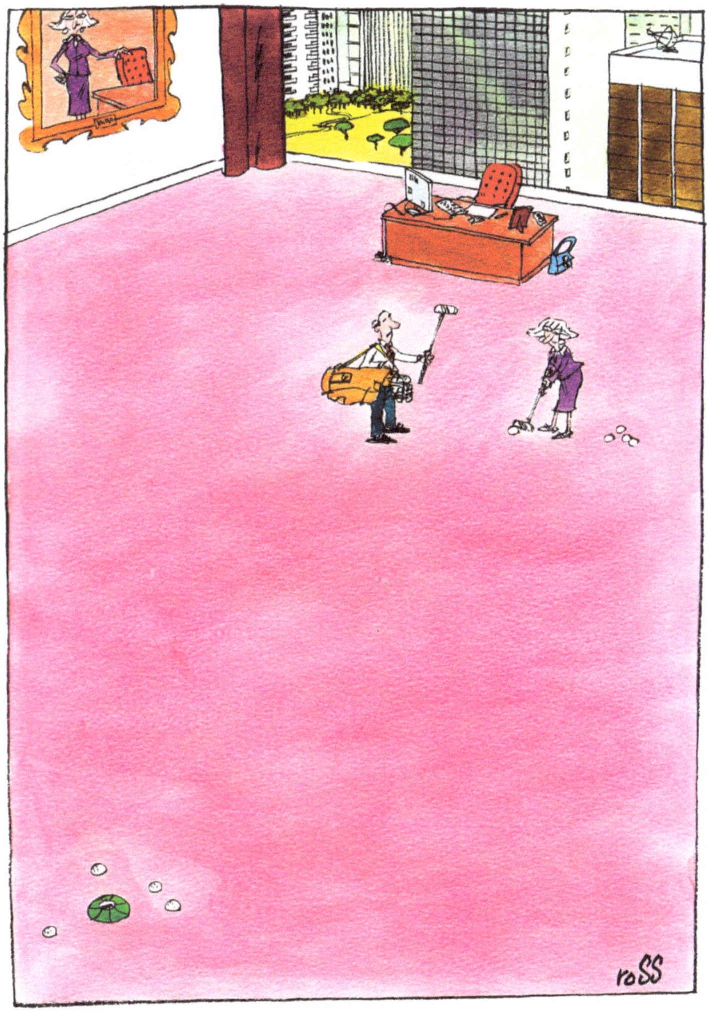
roSS

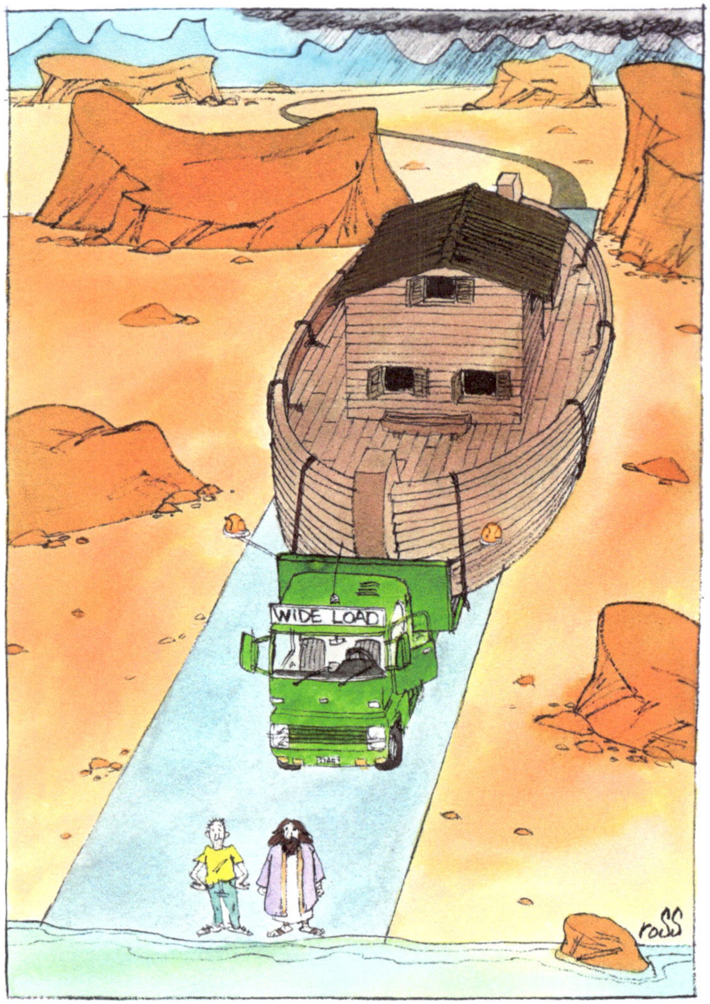
WIDE LOAD
roSS

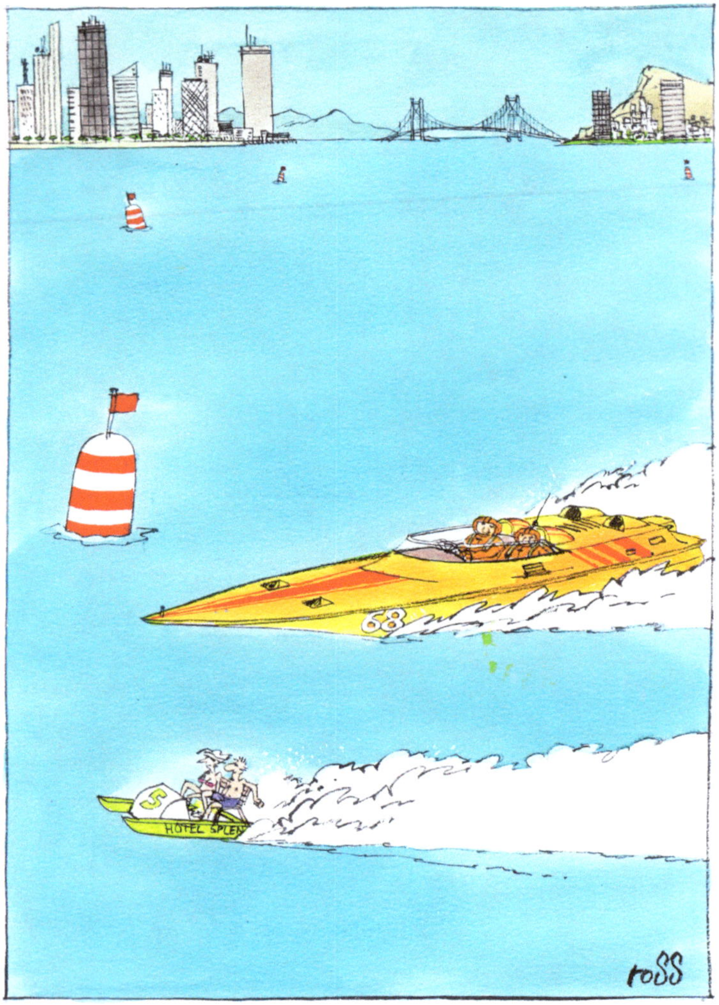
68
5
HOTEL SPLEN
roSS

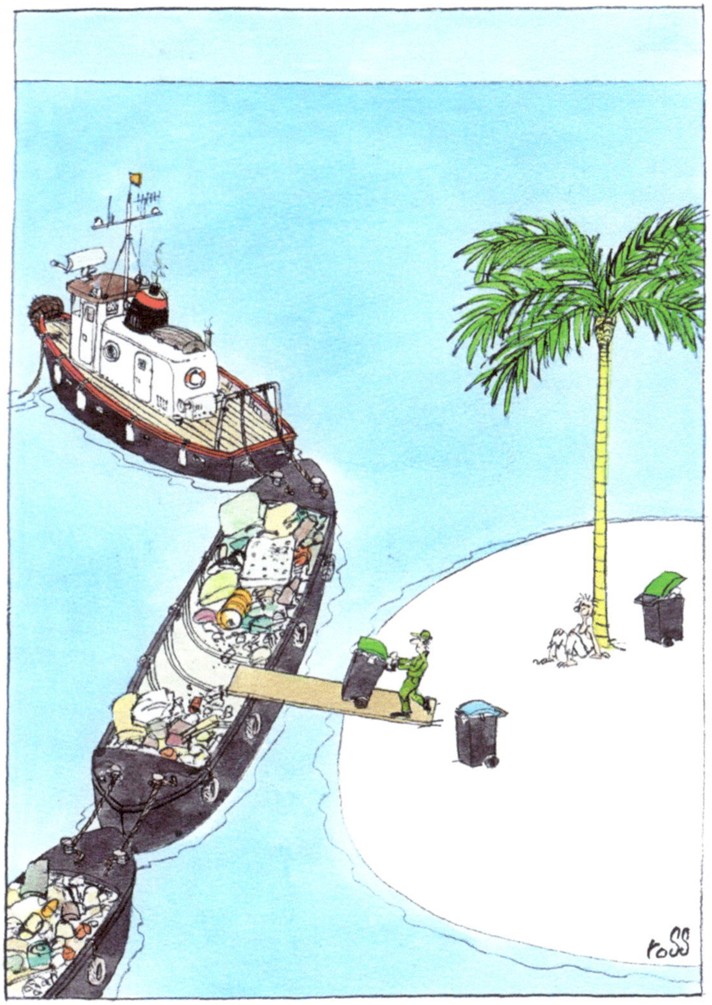
roSS
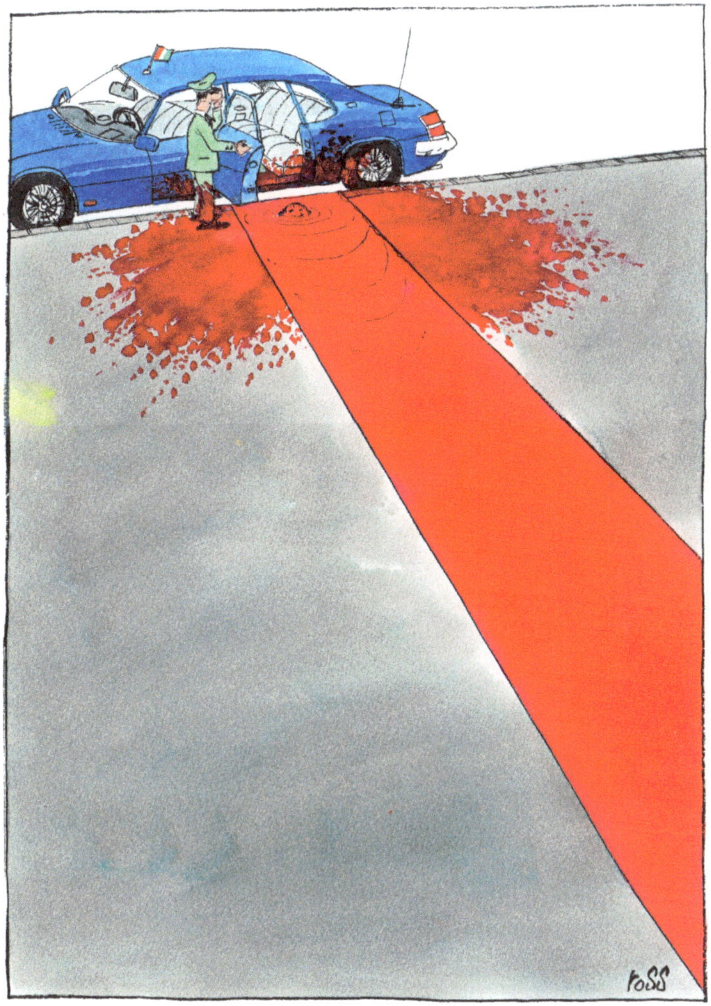
roSS

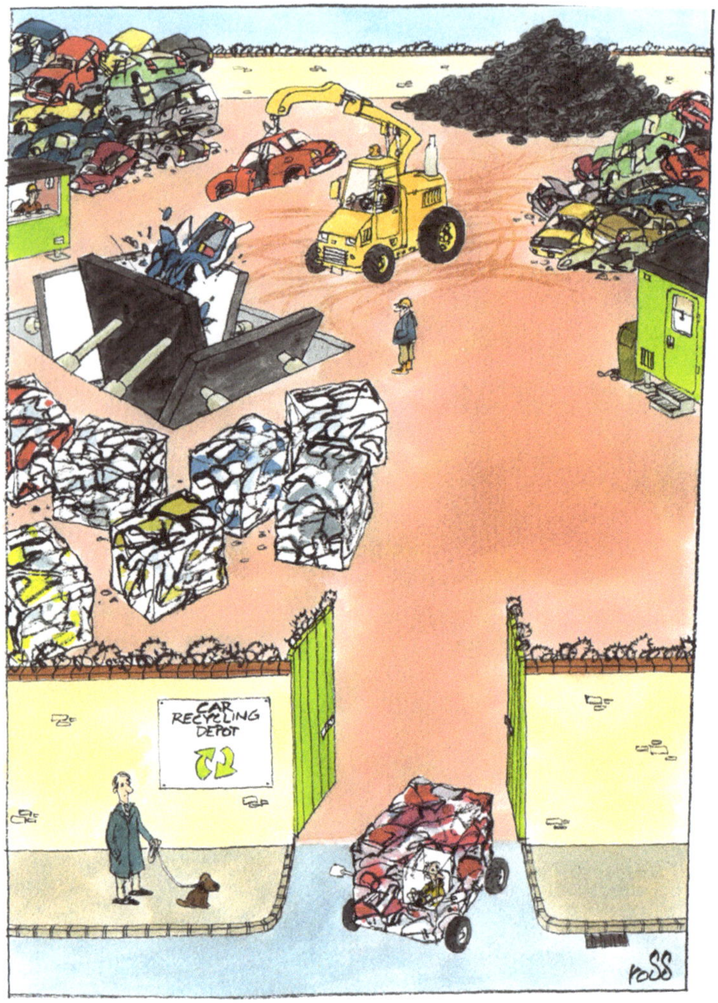
CAR RECYCLING DEPOT
ross

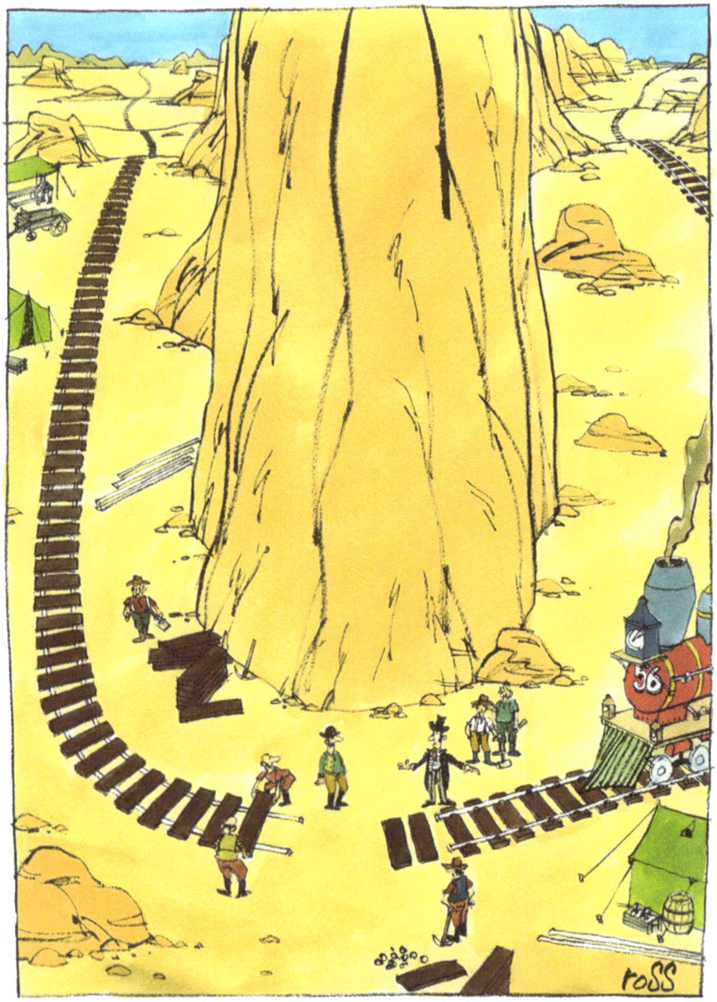
56
ross

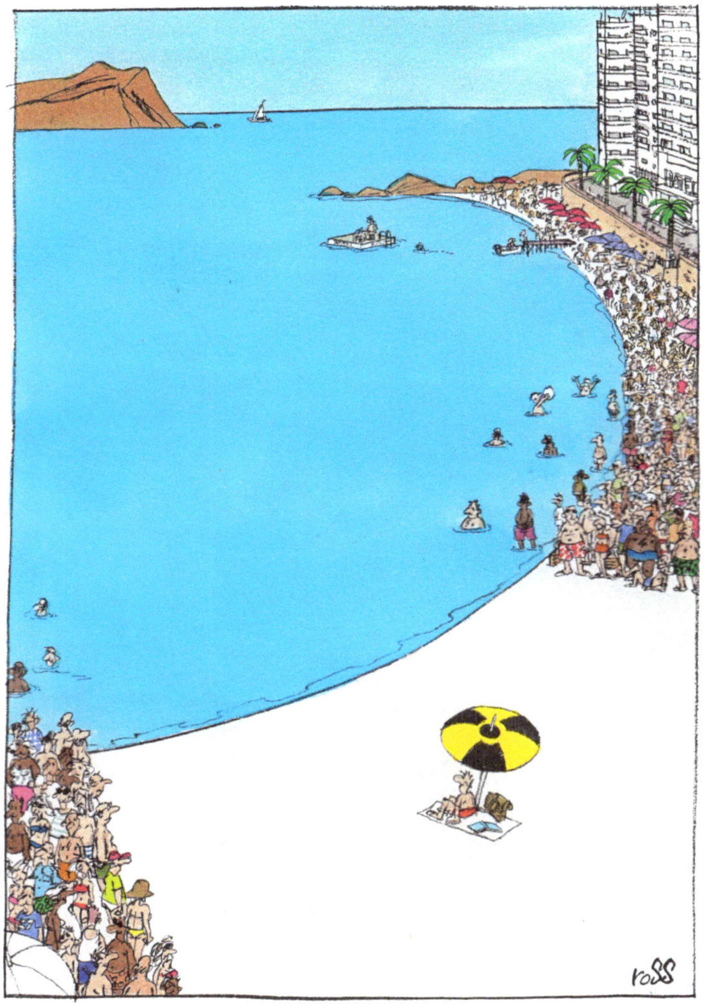
roSS

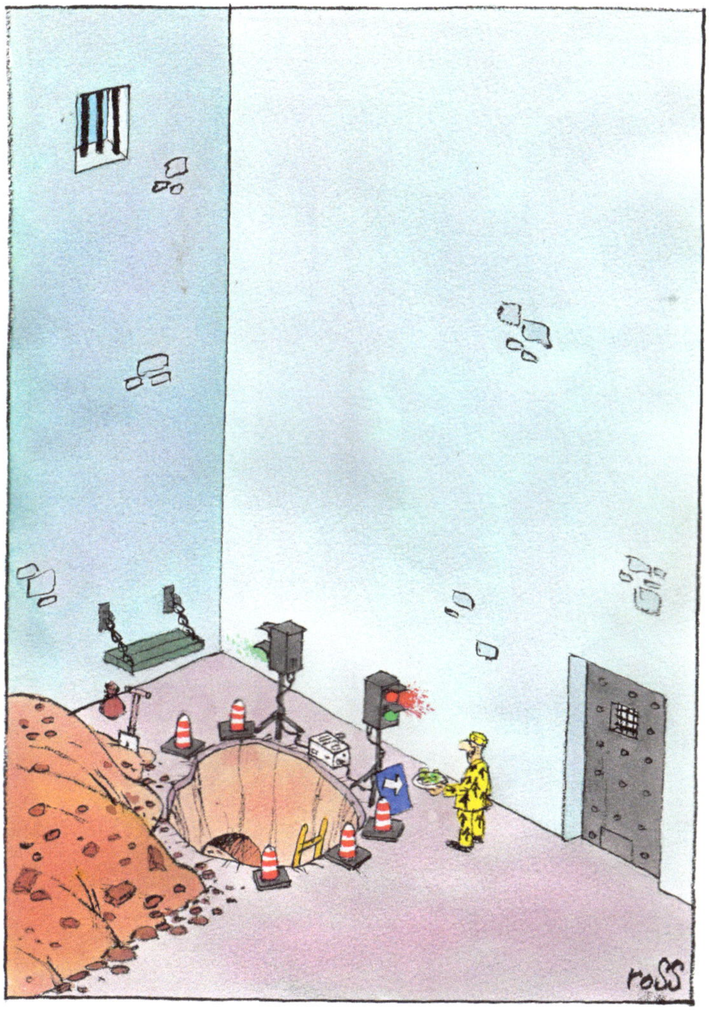
roSS

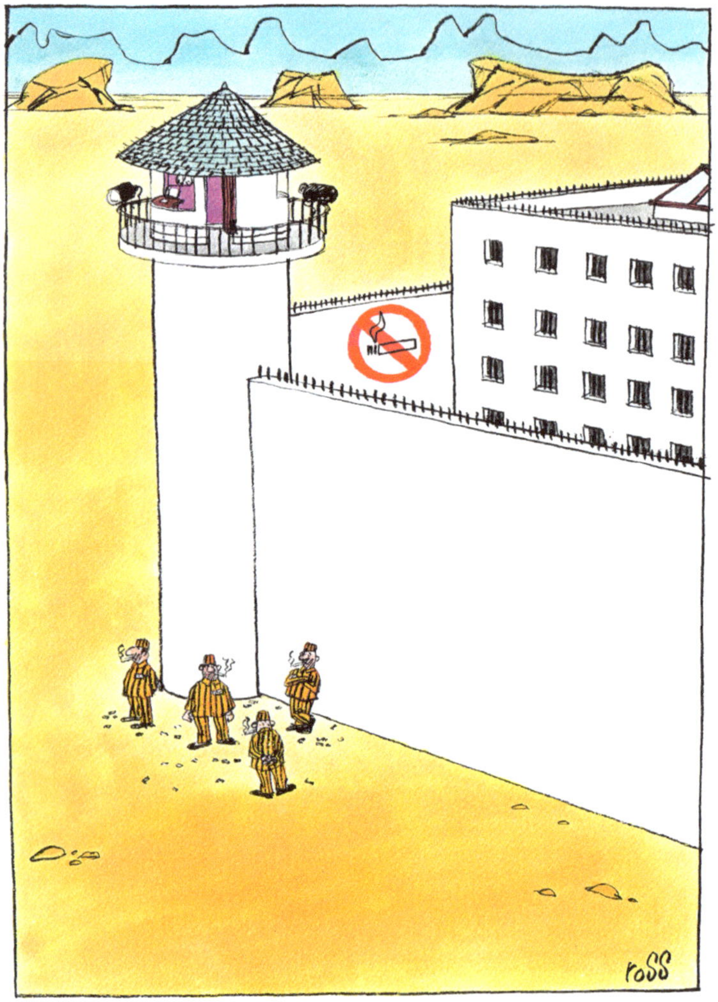
roSS

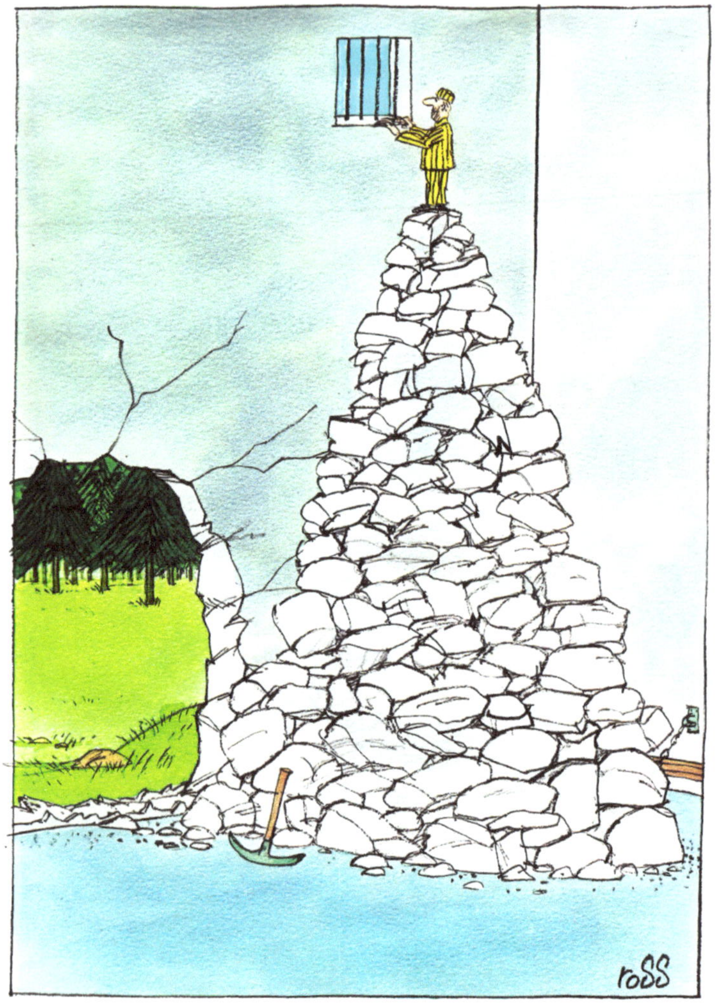
roSS

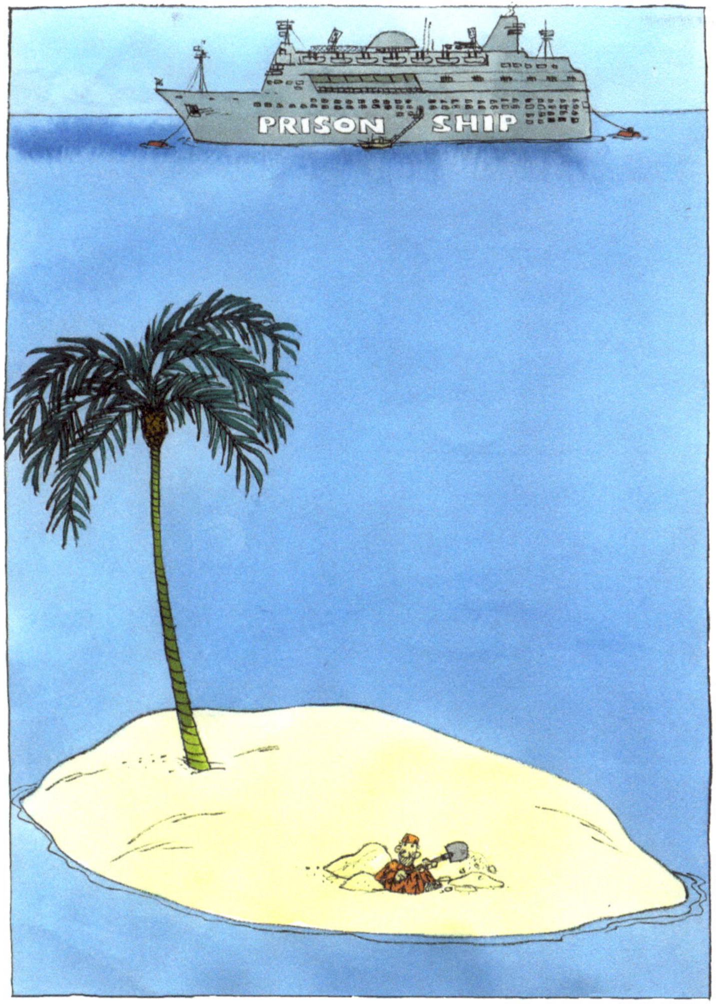
PRISON SHIP

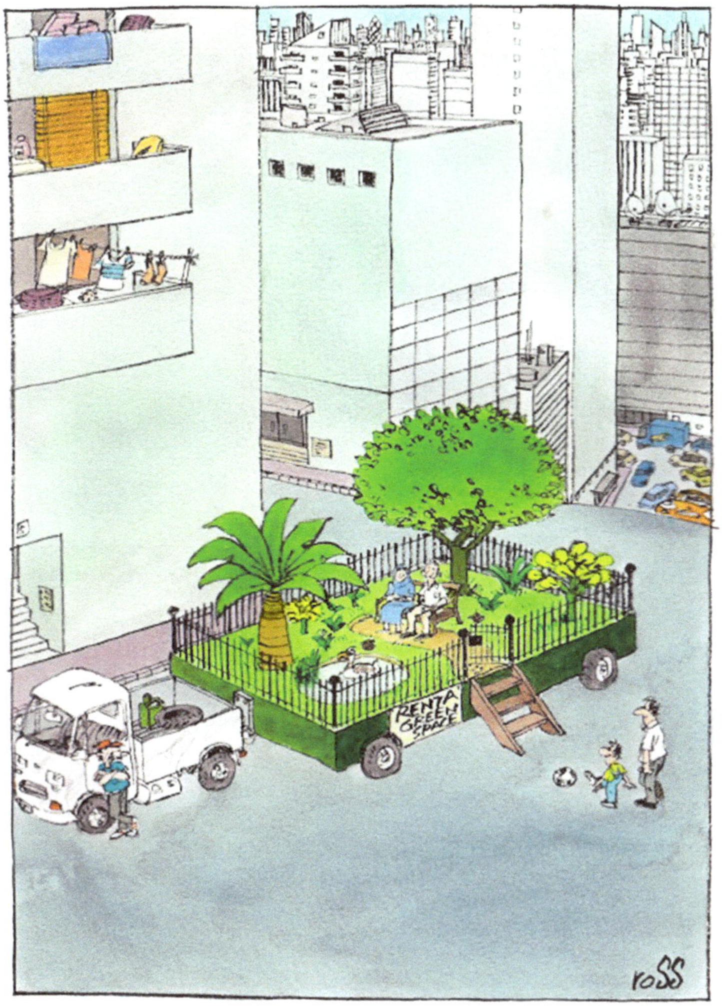
RENTA GREEN SPACE
roSS

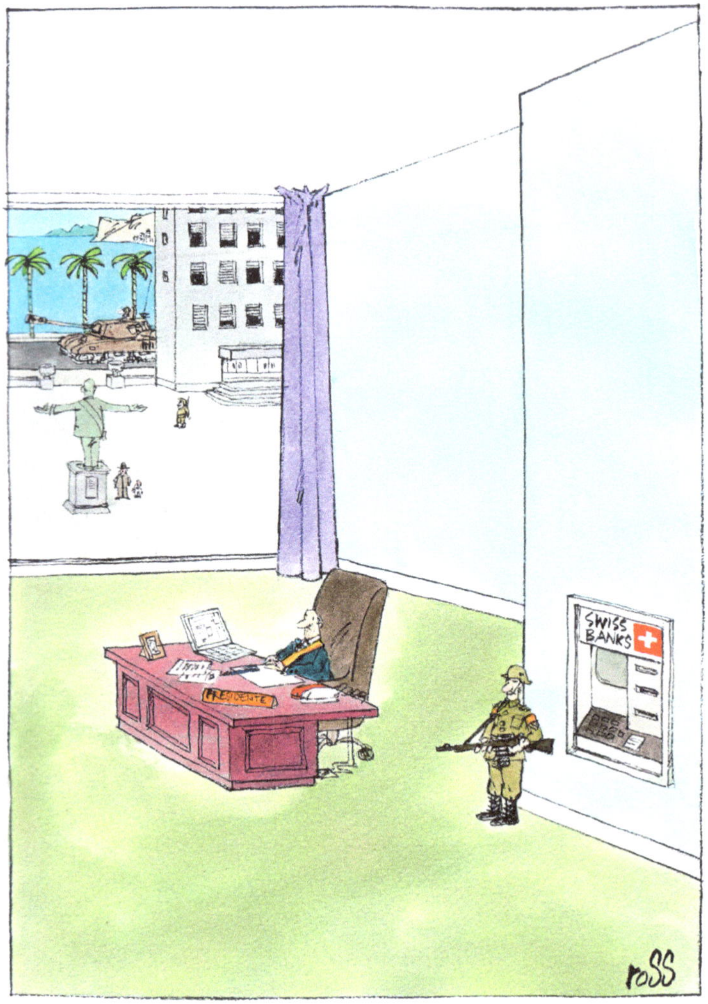
SWISS
BANKS
roSS

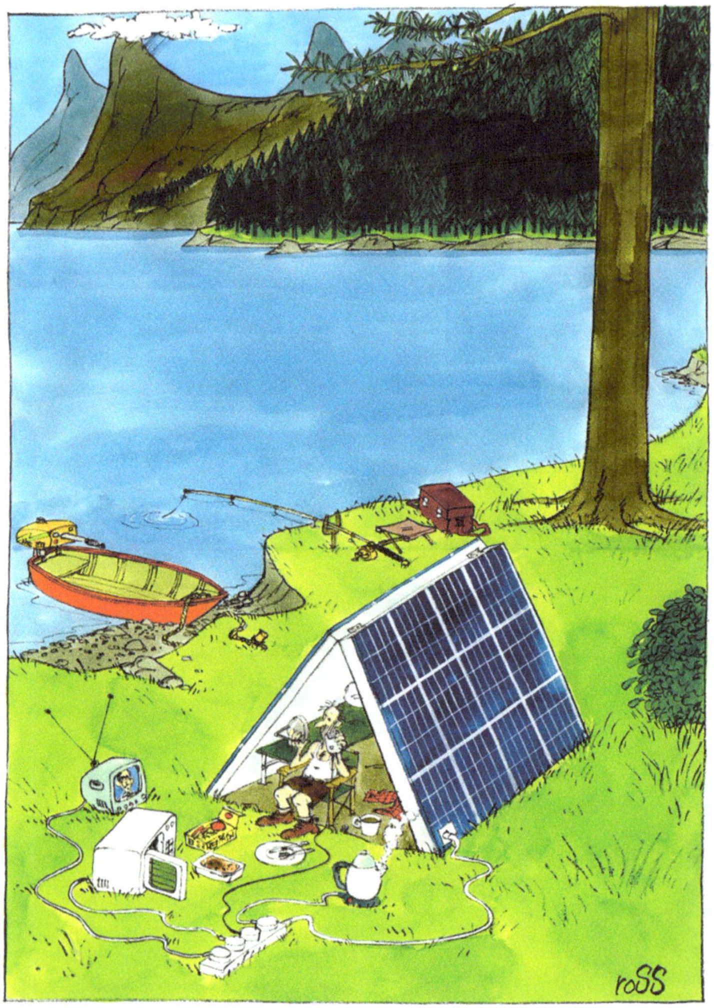
roSS

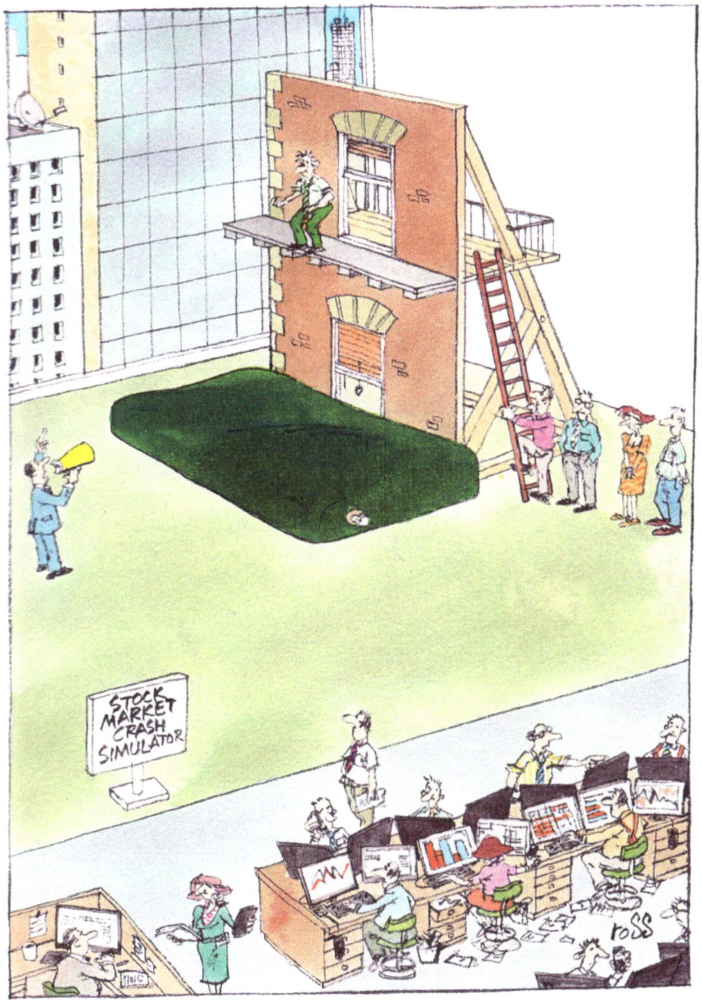
STOCK MARKET CRASH SIMULATOR
ross

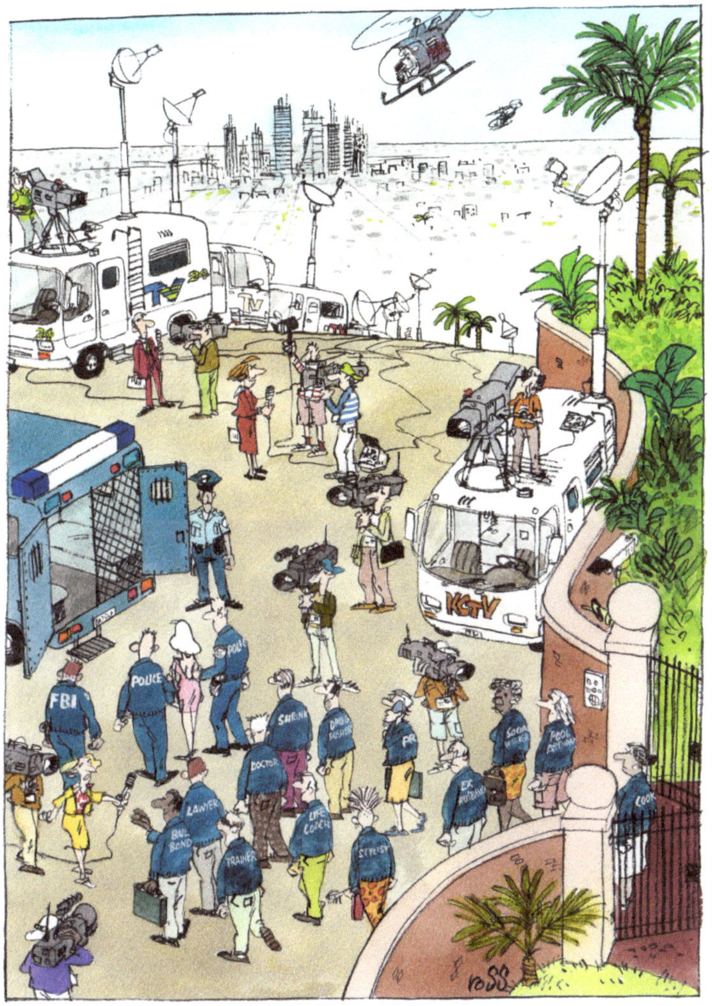
TV
KGTV
FBI
POLICE
POLICE
SHRINK
DRUG PUSHER
PR
SOCIAL WORKER
POOL ATTENDANT
DOCTOR
LAWYER
BAIL BOND
TRAINER
LIFE COACH
STYLIST
EX HUSBAND
COOK
ross

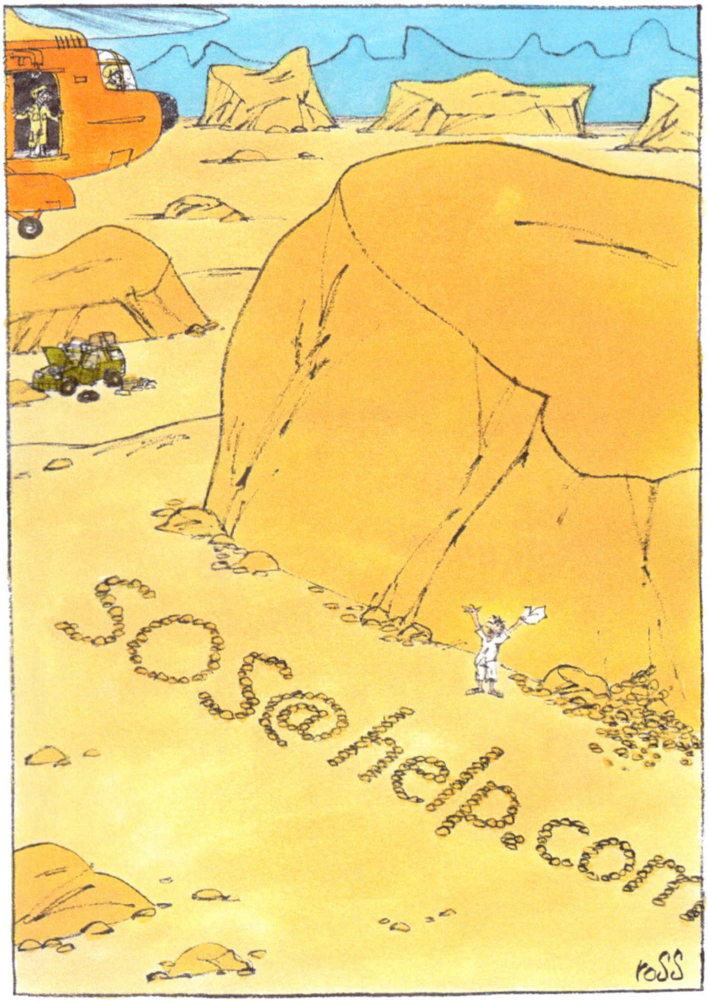
sos@help.com
roSS

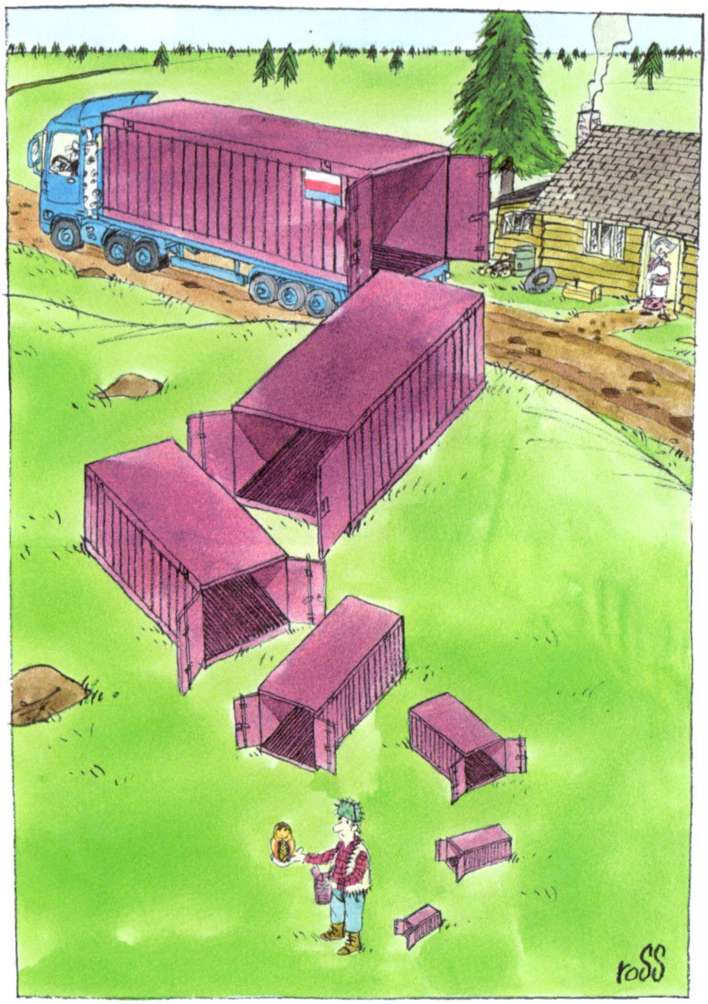
roSS

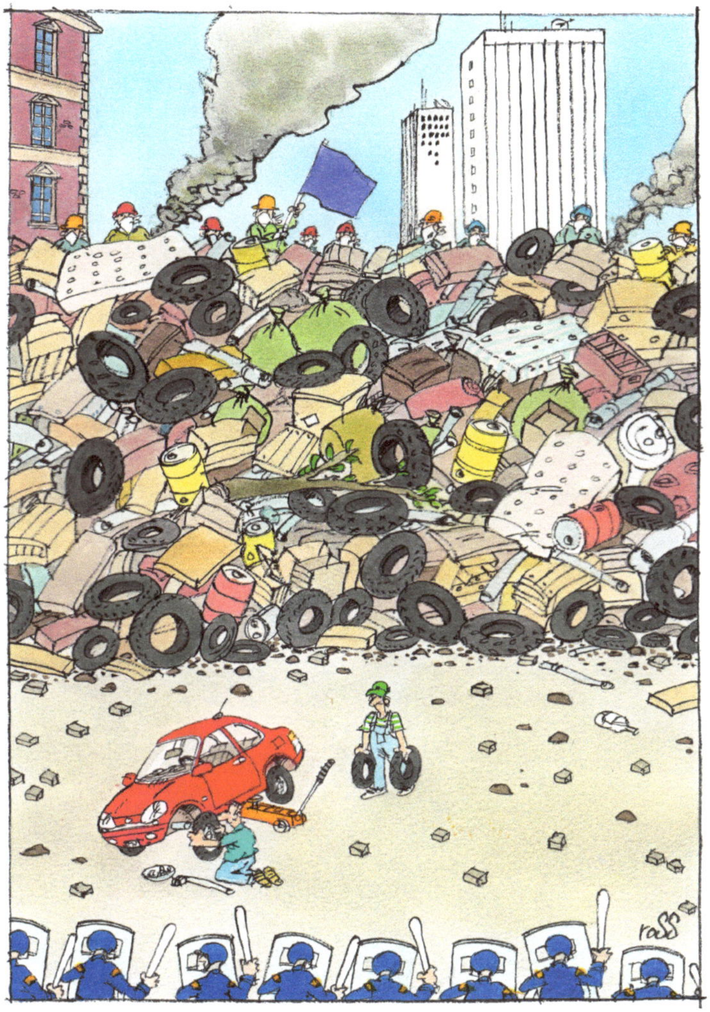
roSS

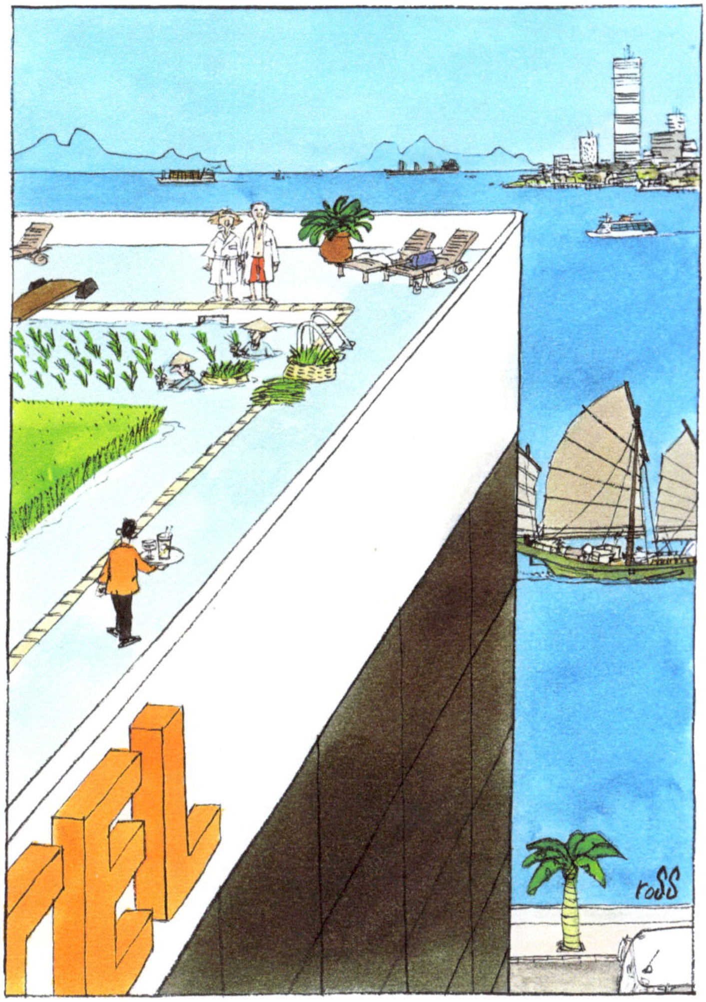
roSS

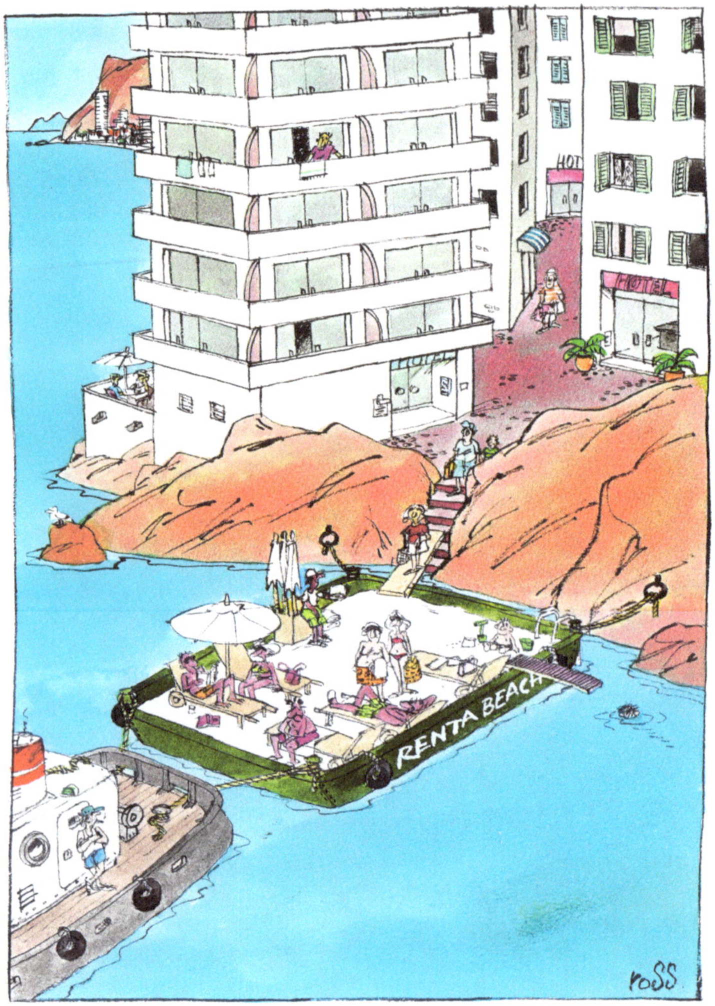
HOTEL
RENTA BEACH
ross

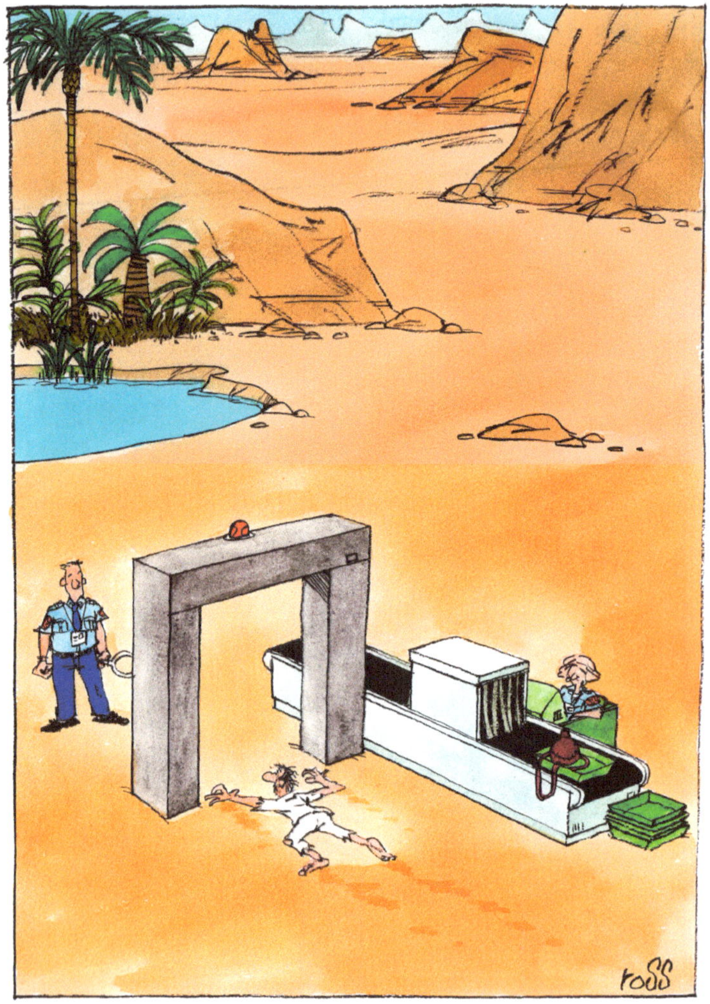
ross

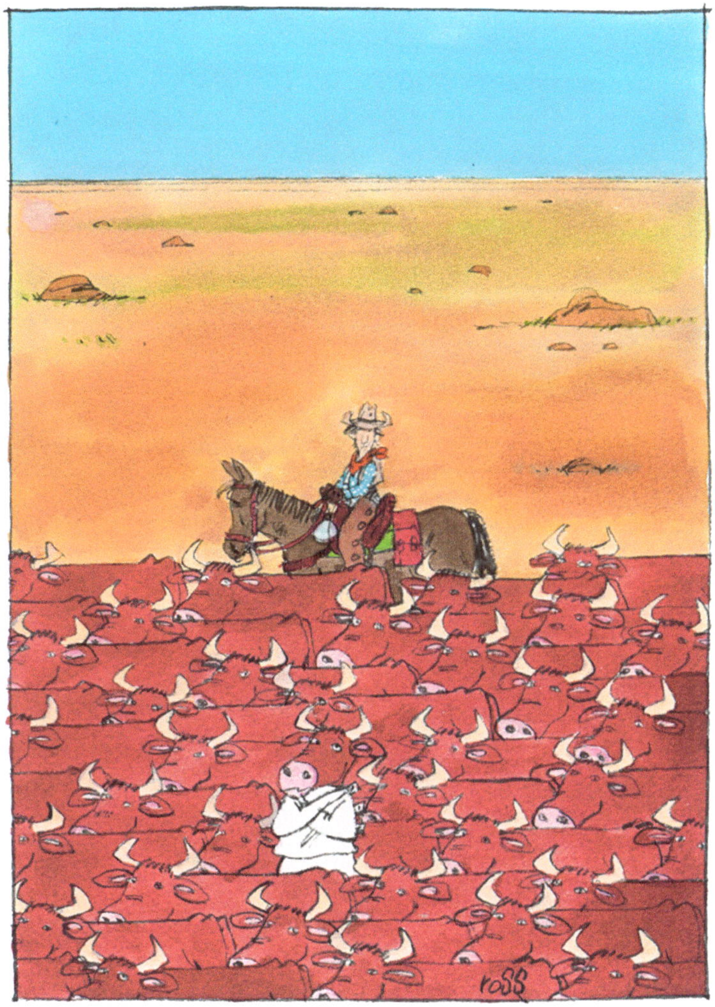
roSS

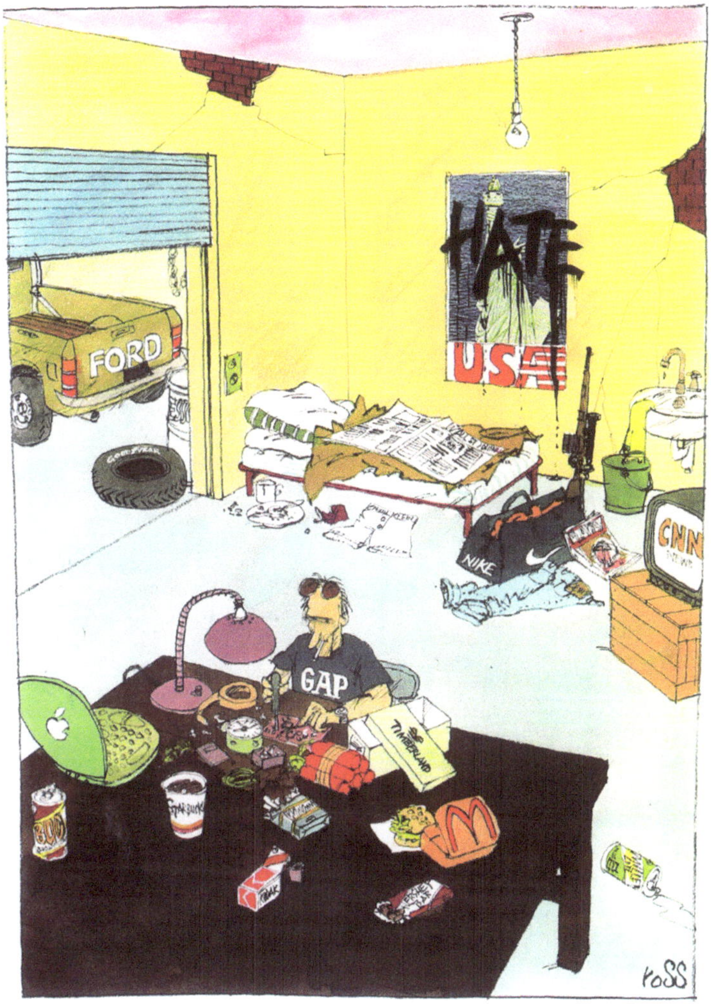
FORD
HATE
USA
NIKE
CNN
GAP
TIMBERLAND
roSS

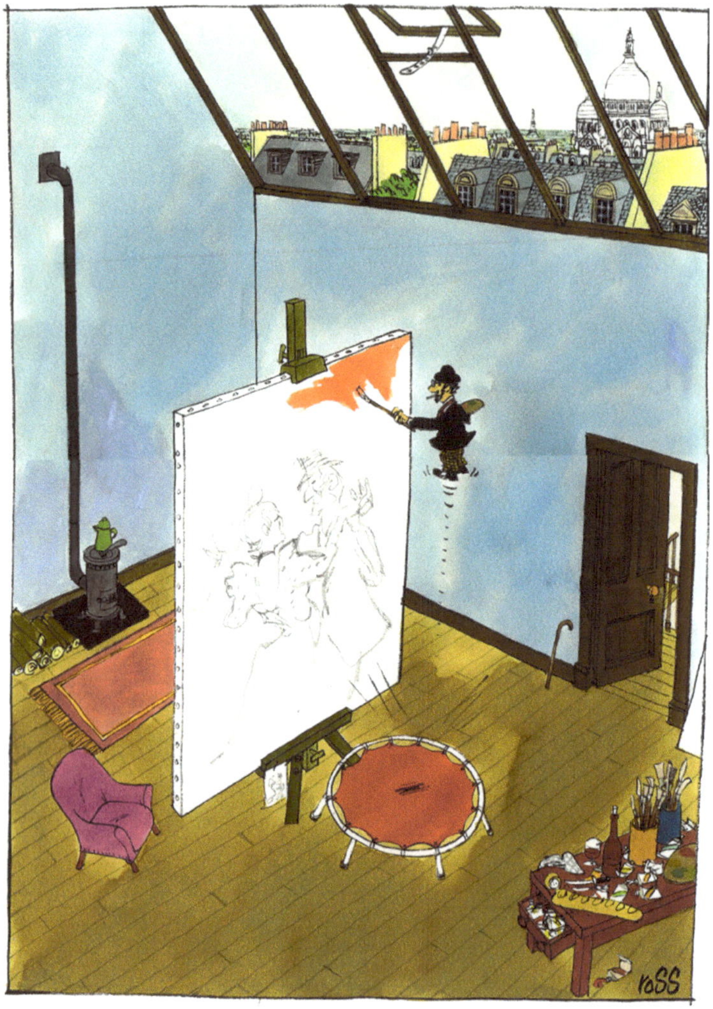
roSS

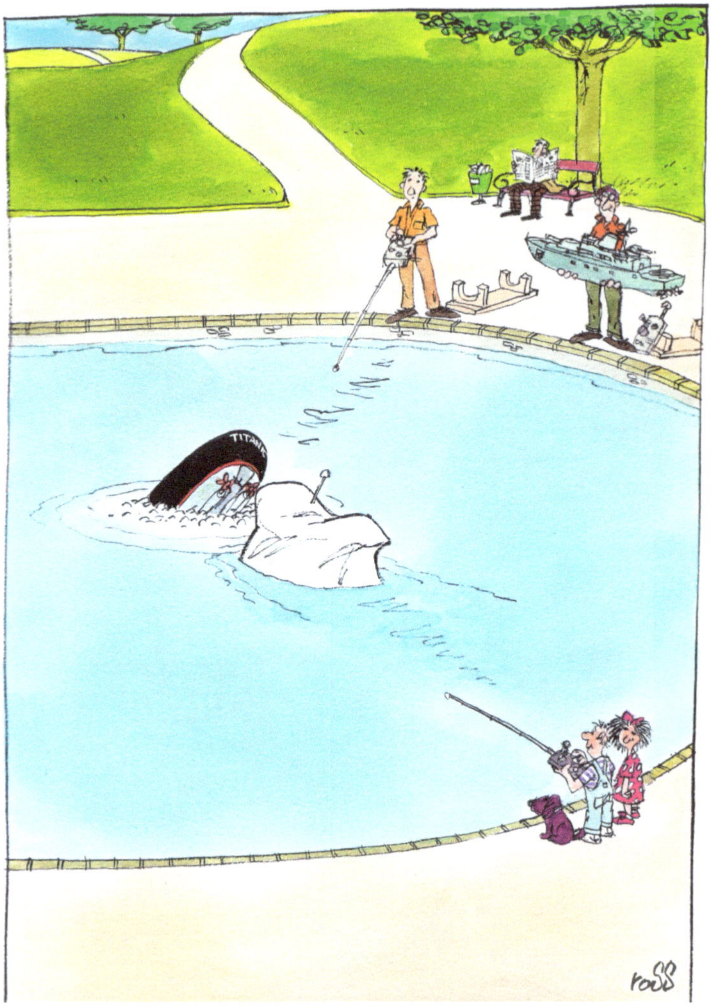
TITANIC
roSS

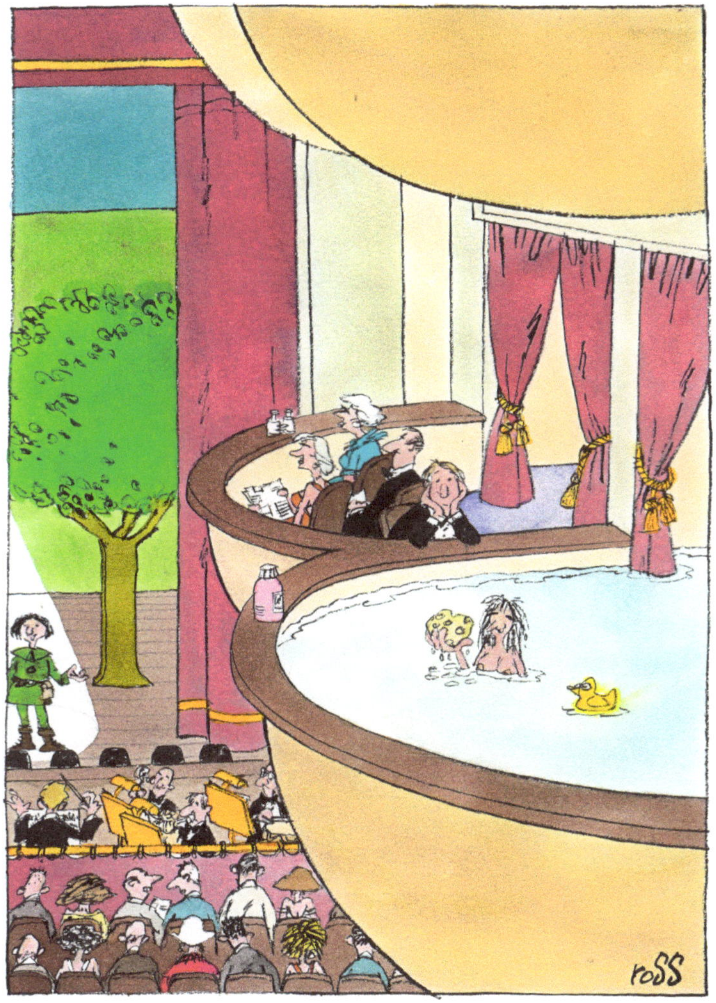
roSS

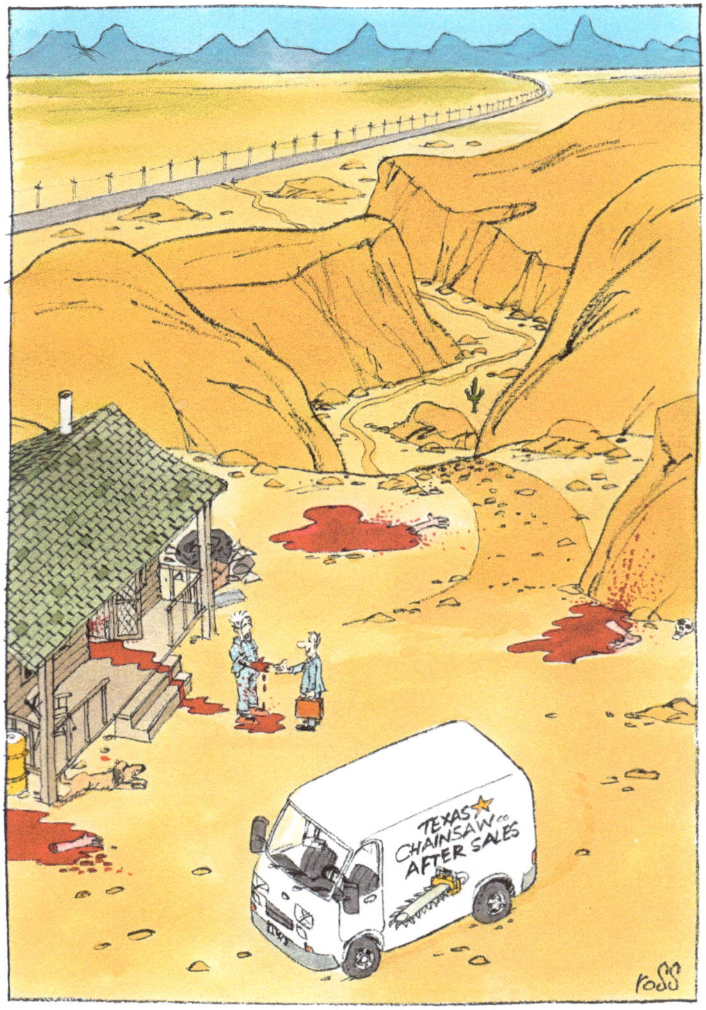
TEXAS CHAINSAW Co
AFTER SALES
roSS

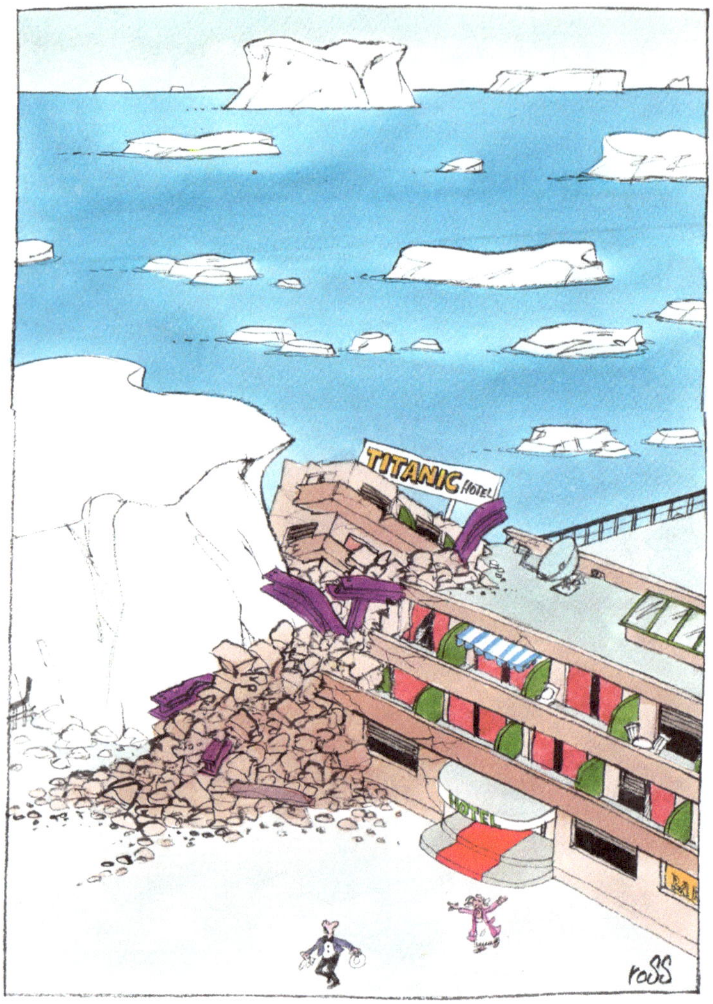
TITANIC HOTEL
HOTEL
roSS

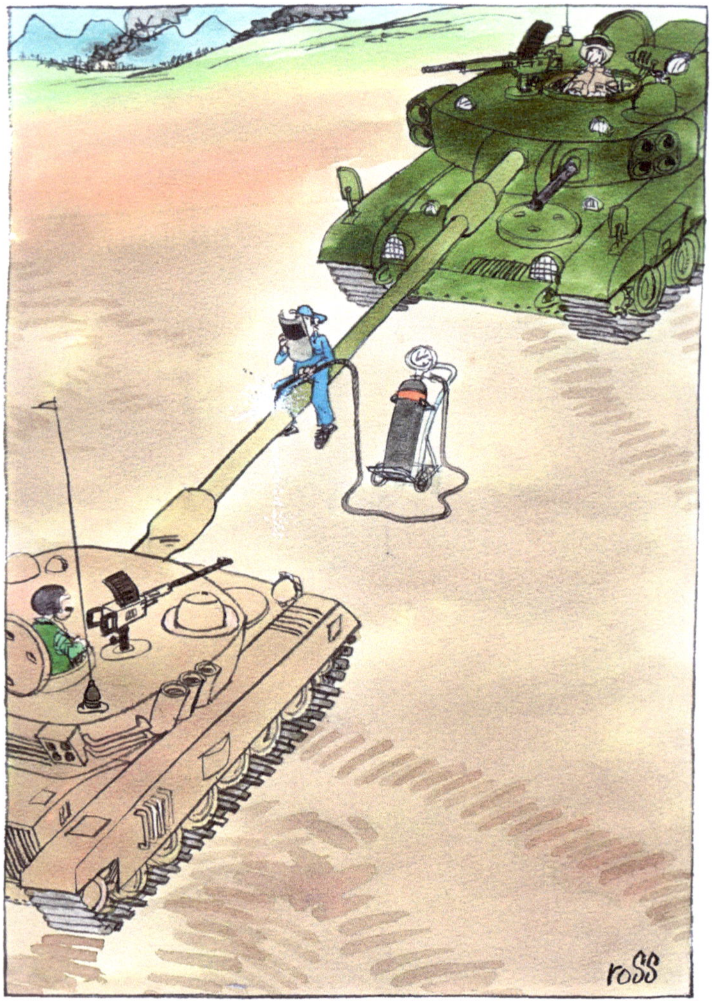
roSS

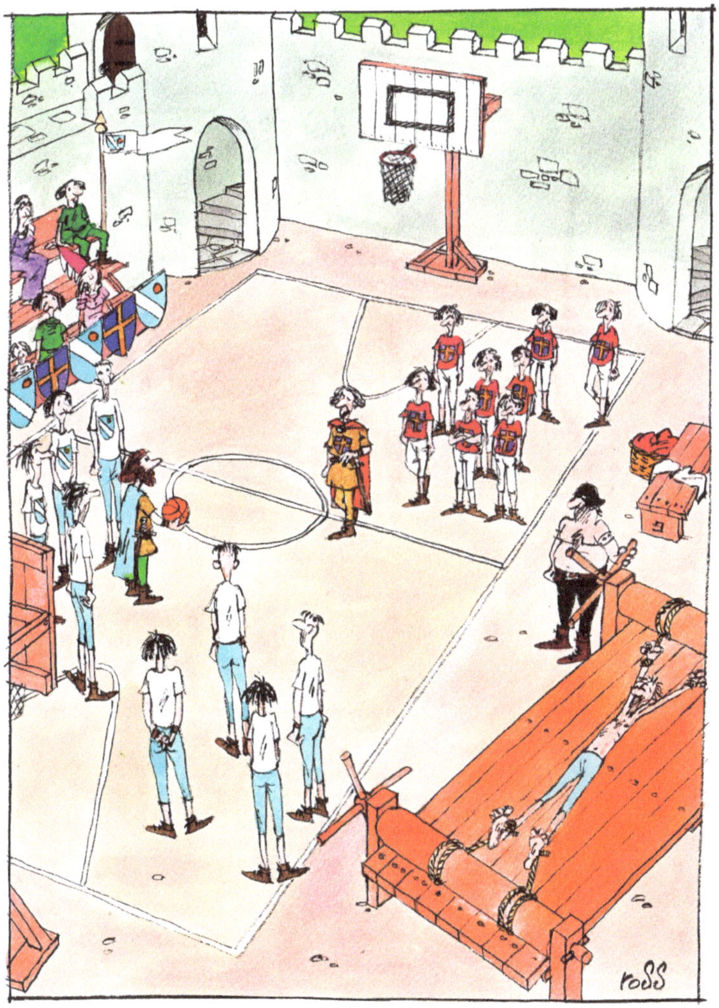
roSS

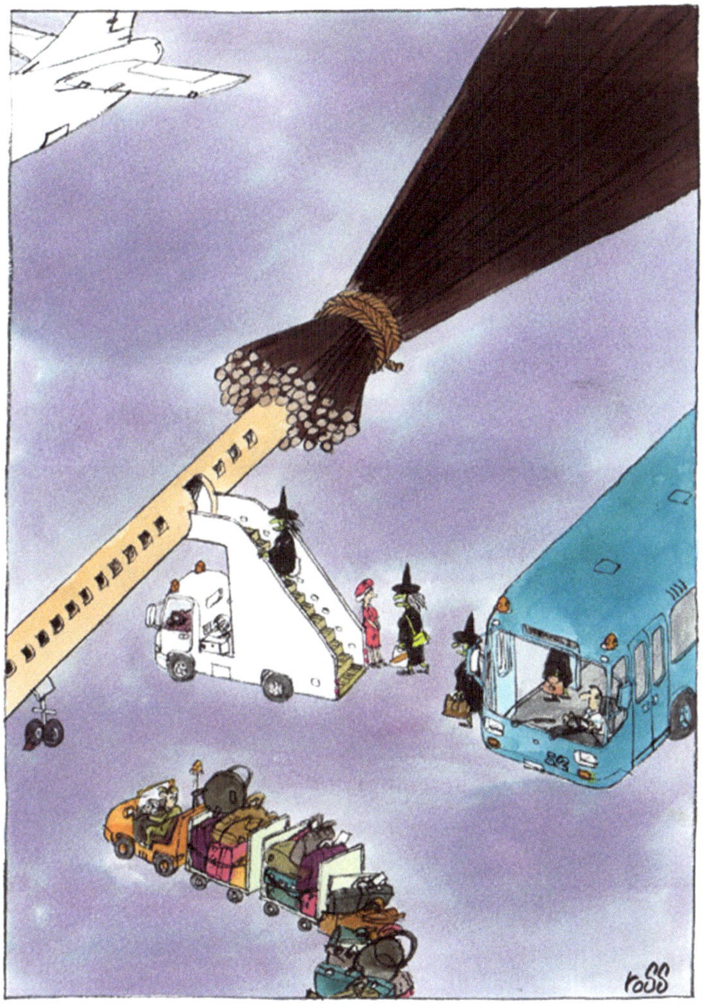
roSS

roSS
cartoons

www.ingramcontent.com/pod-product-compliance
Lightning Source LLC
Chambersburg PA
CBHW051217220526
45473CB00003B/1067
9798507510726